Praise for Shifra Stein's *Day*

Day Trips from Kansas City:

"A slim little volume of history, foods, fun and vacation information."—*The Squire*

"This book contains something for everyone."—*Olathe Daily News*

"Day Trips is crammed with mini-vacation ideas that let you roam to your heart's delight on a shoestring budget."—*Kansas City Star*

". . . describes over 200 exciting places to visit in Kansas and Missouri, less than two hours from Kansas City and easily reached on a tank or two of gas." —*Kansas Magazine*

"The book is well thought out and creatively presented, with much of the skill demonstrated by Ms. Stein in her newspaper work."—*The Kansas City Jewish Chronicle*

Day Trips from Phoenix, Tucson, and Flagstaff:

"Presents a diversity of explorations including Indian Ruins, ghost towns, lost mines and artist colonies."—*The Los Angeles Times*

Day Trips from Houston:

"A feisty little guide featuring an assortment of intriguing excursions within 2 hours driving time of Houston."—*The Orange Leader*

Day Trips from Baltimore:

"After you've read this book, you may want to schedule that next visit to history land to Baltimore, rather than Washington, D.C."—*Chattanooga News-Free Press*

Day Trips from Cincinnati:

". . . a highly readable, usable book for the summer or any time of year."—*The Cincinnati Enquirer*

SHIFRA STEIN'S

DAY TRIPS®

FROM

SAN ANTONIO
AND
AUSTIN

TWO LANE PRESS, INC.

Books by Shifra Stein:
Day Trips from Kansas City
Kansas City Cuisine (coauthored with Karen Adler)
Kansas City Guide

First printing April 1992

Day Trips® is a registered trademark.

ISBN: 1-878686-04-6

Printed in the United States of America

Cover design: Jim Langford
Cover illustration: Brad Springer
Editing and text design: Jane Doyle Guthrie
Maps: Gayland Burke

10   9   8   7   6   5   4   3   93   94   95   96

Two Lane Press, Inc.
4245 Walnut
Kansas City, Missouri 64111

Contents

Preface

Most people have a mental image of Texas as miles of rugged, uncivilized land where the outlines of cattle and lonely windmills stretch above the horizon. But that's just one side of this Lone Star State known as the "land of contrast." Texas also boasts high-tech cities, piney woods, sandy beaches, rolling hills, and fertile farmland—much of it within a two-hour drive of San Antonio and Austin.

The region covered in this book is as diverse as the more than 30 cultures who helped found the state. German, French, Mexican, Polish, and even Alsatian settlers brought their traditions to Texas in the 1800s. The influences of these pioneers are still apparent today in the varied festivals and ethnic foods that vacationers come here to enjoy.

The day trips within this book span terrain ranging from farmland to rocky hills. This difference in topography is the result of an ancient earthquake that created the Balcones Fault, which runs north to south. The fault line, slightly west of I-35, forms the dividing line between the eastern agricultural region and what is known as the hill country to the west.

Many of the attractions lie along the route taken by the 350,000 Winter Texans who flock here during the cooler months. So, whether you're heading for the Rio Grande Valley, the coast, or the Mexican border, you'll find a wealth of useful tips and information in this guide. Be sure to check the sections marked "Especially for Winter Texans." This will help you identify special services, festivals, or parks aimed at making you feel right at home.

You'll find that Texans are friendly folk who wave on country roads and nod as they pass you on the sidewalk. Talk to local citizens as you wind through the back roads for even more travel tips and a first-hand look at the varied cultures that make up the pieces of your journey.

Texas Travel Tips

CARRY A ROAD MAP

Although we've included directions, it's best to carry a Texas road map as you travel. It's also advisable to carry a county map for a better look at farm-to-market (FM) and ranch roads (RR). You can get brochures on Texas attractions and a free copy of the "Texas State Travel Guide" from the the the State Department of Highways and Public Transportation, P.O. Box 5064, Austin, TX 78763, or by calling (800) 8888-TEX. The guide is coded to a free Texas state map also provided by the Highway Department. These maps are also available from any of the 12 Tourist Information Centers located on routes into Texas and at the Texas State Capitol in Austin. The Travel Information Centers are open daily, except for Thanksgiving, Christmas, and New Year's Day.

The expansiveness of Texas sets it apart from other states. Note the scale of the map. With 266,807 square miles of land, Texas is the second largest state in the country. One inch on the state road map spans 23 miles.

Driving varies with terrain: The two-hour time limit that constitutes a "day trip" here has been stretched for the westernmost trips in this book. You won't find many towns en route from San Antonio to the Mexican border, and there's little traffic to slow your drive. To the east, population is more dense, and day trips involve quiet, slow drives along farm-to-market (FM) and ranch roads (RR).

CARRY EXTRA FOOD AND WATER

Once you're on a back road, you'll be heading into Texas-sized landscape that isn't always easy to navigate. Distances may be deceiving, and sometimes there are no places to stop along the way. When planning your day trip, always carry extra water and a nonperishable lunch. This way you can enjoy the sweeping vista before you with a pleasant roadside picnic.

In summer, the Texas heat is hotter than sizzling fajitas. *Always* carry water in your car for emergencies: you may need it for drinking or cooling down an overheated engine. In warm weather, it's best to drive in the early morning hours or after sunset. And if you really plan to wander about, always tell someone when you plan to return.

HEED ROAD SIGNS AND WEATHER WARNINGS

Always be on the lookout for road signs, and if you see a notice, observe it. Obey flash flood warnings: A sudden rainstorm can turn a wash into a deadly torrent. Never cross a flooded roadway; it may be deeper than you think.

WATCH OUT FOR STRAY LIVESTOCK

When driving through open-ranch cattle country on farm-to-market or ranch roads, be on the lookout for livestock and deer wandering across the road, especially near dusk.

USING THIS TRAVEL GUIDE

Highway designations: Federal highways are designated US. State routes use TX for Texas. Farm-to-market roads are defined as FM, and ranch roads are labeled RR. County roads (which are not on the Texas state map) are identified as county roads.

Hours: In most cases, hours are omitted in the listings because they are subject to frequent changes. Instead, phone numbers are provided for obtaining up-to-date information.

Restaurants: Restaurant prices are designated as $$$ (Expensive: $15 and over); $$ (Moderate: $5–15); and $ (Inexpensive: $5 and under).

Accommodations: Room prices are designated as $$$ (Expensive: over $100 for a standard room); $$ (Moderate: $50–100); and $ (Inexpensive: under $50).

Credit cards: The symbol [] denotes that credit cards are accepted.

Day Trips from San Antonio

Welcome to San Antonio, the Alamo City and the gateway to South Texas. Boasting a semitropical climate, San Antonio is a city of lush vegetation, offering a south of the border atmosphere with north of the border amenities.

San Antonio lies at the juncture of the hill country, farmland, and brush country that stretches to the Mexican border. Because it's in the middle of such geographic diversity, San Antonio has a wealth of day trips awaiting you. You can head to the urban areas of Austin or Corpus Christi, or to small towns where it's not uncommon to hear German, Czech, Spanish, or even Alsatian spoken on the street. You also can get away from it all with a quiet walk along miles of undeveloped beach on Padre Island, or take a bird-watching cruise along the intracoastal waterway of the Rockport-Fulton area.

Many day trips include information about overnight accommodations to make your visit more relaxing and unhurried. And don't forget to leave plenty of time for watching a king-sized Texas sunset or sunrise over the Gulf waters.

For brochures and maps on San Antonio area attractions, call (800) 447-3372 or (210) 270-8700, or write: San Antonio Convention and Visitors Bureau, P.O. Box 2277, San Antonio, TX 78298.

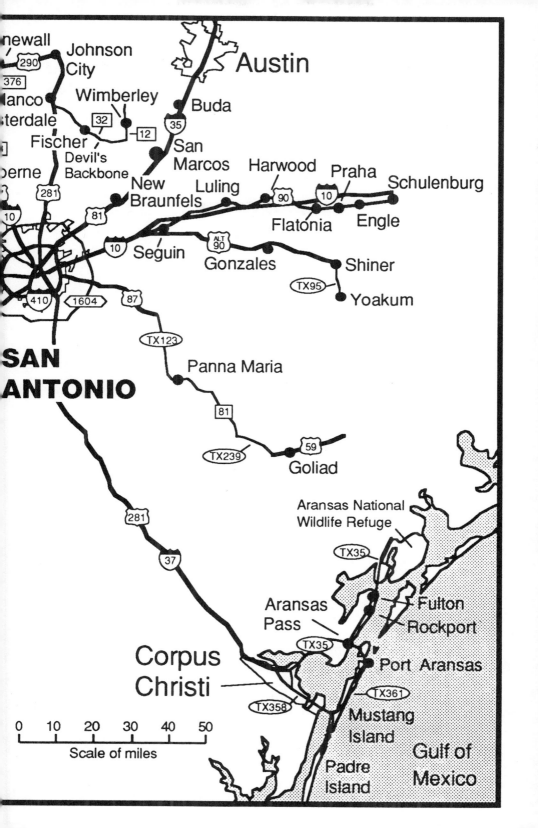

Day Trip 1

BLANCO
FISCHER
DEVIL'S BACKBONE SCENIC DRIVE
WIMBERLEY

BLANCO

To reach Blanco, follow US 281 north of San Antonio past miles of cattle ranches and hill country vistas. Formerly a "Wild West" kind of town, the community was the county seat of Blanco County back in 1886. Although the county seat eventually was moved to nearby Johnson City, where it remains today, local residents are hard at work restoring Blanco's old limestone courthouse as a museum and art gallery.

Around the courthouse square are several art galleries and antique shops aimed at weekend visitors, many of whom stop to camp at the Blanco River State Recreation Area south of town.

WHERE TO GO

Blanco River State Recreation Area. South of Blanco on US 281. During the Depression, the Civilian Conservation Corps built two stone dams, a group pavilion, stone picnic tables, and an arched bridge in this riverside park. Today it's popular with swimmers, fishermen, and campers. Fee. (210) 833-4333.

Shrine of the Blessed Virgin Mary. At Christ of the Hills Monastery. Turn left off US 281 at the Blanco River State Recreation Area, then follow County Road 102 across the river for two miles. Turn at the "Clear Spring Ranch" gate (County Road 103) and continue for 2½ miles.

The Christ of the Hills Monastery houses an order of Eastern Orthodox monks and nuns who practice a religion similar to the Russian Orthodox, except that services are conducted in English.

Budget about an hour for a tour of the chapel and a look at the weeping icon. Painted in 1983 by a California monk, the icon is a representation of Mary and Jesus. After two years in its Blanco location, the icon began to weep myrrh. Drops of the oil roll from the eyes of both the mother and child. According to the

4

inhabitants of the monastery, the painting weeps intermittently, although the oily streaks of the tears can be seen at almost any time. The myrrh is caught in cotton balls at the base of the icon, and visitors are anointed with the fragrant oil after viewing the painting.

The monastery is open to all, regardless of faith. Tours are conducted daily during the summer, and Thursday through Monday during the rest of the year. Sunday tours are given at 1 p.m. Appropriate dress is required; shorts are not allowed. Women are asked to cover their heads; scarves are provided. Free. (210) 833-5363.

Blanco Bowling Club. East of the square on Fourth St. Housed in 1940s buildings, the bowling club and the adjacent cafe have changed little with the passing years. The nine-pin game is still set up by hand as it has been for generations. The bowling club opens at 7:30 p.m., Monday through Friday (except during football season, when everyone's at the Friday night high school game). To bowl you must be a member, but the general public is free to join. Fee. (210) 833-4416.

WHERE TO SHOP

Rainbird Gallery. US 281 (Main St.). Blanco is home to many well-known artists who've relocated here from around the country. One artist, Janet Fisher, owns and operates this art gallery, an eclectic collection of Southwest, Indian, Western, and Texas art. She also sells Navajo rugs, carved fossil rocks, wood and bronze sculptures, and silver jewelry. Paintings include a large selection of scenes of Texas bluebonnets, the state flower. If you call ahead, the owner can arrange a personal tour of the collection. Closed Wednesdays and Sundays. (210) 833-4545 or 833-4983.

WHERE TO EAT

Blanco Bowling Club Cafe. East of the square on Fourth St. This is a traditional Texas diner, with linoleum floor and Formica tables, and chairs filled with locals who come here at the same time every day. Chicken-fried steak is the specialty; on Friday nights there's a catfish plate as well. Stop by in the morning for huge glazed twists and doughnuts made from scratch. Open daily for breakfast, lunch, and dinner. $; no []. (210) 833-4416.

FISCHER

It's just a short, winding drive through the country from Blanco to the tiny hamlet of Fischer. Retrace your drive south on US 281 for a couple of miles to the intersection of RR 32. Take a left and enjoy a quiet ride through miles of ranchland and rolling hills.

Fischer is on the left side of the road. You can't miss the Fischer General

Store. (It's so important, in fact, that the community itself was once called Fischer Store.) Housed in a tin building, here you can buy groceries or mail your postcards—the store also serves as post office, complete with an old-fashioned postmaster's cage and tiny brass mailboxes. Inside, enormous counters span the length of the dark and musty building. Even if you're in a hurry, take five minutes to buy a soft drink and have a look at a part of Texas that's hard to find these days.

DEVIL'S BACKBONE SCENIC DRIVE

The Devil's Backbone scenic drive stretches along RR 32 from Fischer to the intersection of RR 12, your turnoff for Wimberley. There aren't any steep climbs or stomach-churning lookouts; a high ridge of hills provides a gentle drive with excellent views along the way. There's very little traffic, plus a beautiful picnic spot on the left, just a few miles out of Fischer.

WIMBERLEY

At the end of the Devil's Backbone, RR 32 intersects with RR 12. Take a left on RR 12, and drive for five miles. This road drops from the steep ridge to the fertile valley that's home to the Blanco River and Cypress Creek.

The small town of Wimberley is one of those "shop 'til you drop" kind of places. Even with only 7,200 residents, the town boasts dozens of specialty stores, art galleries and studios, and accommodations ranging from river resorts to historic bed and breakfasts.

Wimberley is a quiet place except when the shops open their doors on Fridays, Mondays, and weekends. The busiest time to visit is the first Saturday of the month, from April through November. This is Market Day, when over 400 vendors set up to sell antiques, collectibles, and arts and crafts.

Many visitors come to enjoy the town's two water sources: the Blanco River and clear, chilly Cypress Creek. Both are filled with inner-tubers and swimmers during hot summer months. The waterways provide a temporary home for campers and vacationers who stay in resorts and cabins along the shady water's edge. The most popular swimming spot on Cypress Creek is the Blue Hole Recreation Club, a privately owned park on Old Kyle Road.

WHERE TO GO

Wimberley Chamber of Commerce. Wimberley North Shopping Center, RR 12 past Cypress Creek. Stop by the Chamber offices on weekdays to load up on brochures, maps, and friendly shopping tips. (512) 847-2201.

Pioneer Town. 7-A Ranch Resort, one mile west of RR 12 on County Road

178, at the intersection of County Road 179. See a medicine show, tour a general store museum, or spend some time at the town jail in this Wild West village. There's also a child-sized train ride with a mile of tracks, an old log fort, cowboy shows, and a Western cafe. Open weekends year-round and daily during the summer months. Fee. (512) 847-2517.

Blue Hole Recreation Club. Follow Cypress Creek Rd. and turn left at the cemetery onto Blue Hole Rd. A favorite with locals since the area's pioneer days, this traditional Texas swimming hole comes complete with swinging ropes, tall cypress trees, and the ice-cold water of Cypress Creek. You can stay for the day or camp overnight (rustic or hookup). Fee. (512) 847-9127.

WHERE TO SHOP

Like nearby Blanco, Wimberley is home to many artists who've relocated to Texas's serene hill country. Specialty shops abound, selling everything from imports to sculpture and antiques. Arts and crafts are especially well represented.

Plan to shop Friday through Monday. Some stores are open all week, but most close mid-week, especially during cooler months.

Cypress Creek Gallery. RR 12, downtown. Whether you're looking for a miniature silver cowboy hat or a wall-sized Southwest watercolor, you're probably going to find it here. The enormous gallery also sells stone sculpture, ceramics, and Indian kachina dolls.

Billie Bob's Knob. Two miles north of Wimberley on RR 12. This is Wimberley's largest store, a 12-room shopping extravaganza sprawled over 6,000 square feet. Antiques, designer clothing, jewelry, home furnishings, and collectibles are offered for sale. (512) 847-3379.

WHERE TO STAY

Bed and Breakfast of Wimberley. This reservation service can place you in host homes in town, on Cypress Creek, and on area ranches. They inspect the accommodations prior to rental. (512) 847-9666 or 847-2837.

Wimberley Lodging. Bed and breakfasts, rental homes, condominiums, resorts, hotels, and area camps are handled by this central reservation service. For information, call (800) 725-3909, or write: P.O. Box 1807, Wimberley, TX 78676.

For a brochure on Wimberley's many accommodations, call the Wimberley Chamber of Commerce at (512) 847-2201.

Day Trip 2

JOHNSON CITY
STONEWALL
LUCKENBACH
FREDERICKSBURG
ENCHANTED ROCK STATE PARK

JOHNSON CITY

The Lyndon B. Johnson National Historic Park takes in two areas: Johnson City and the LBJ Ranch. To reach Johnson City, follow US 281 north to Blanco (see NORTH FROM SAN ANTONIO, DAY TRIP 1 in this section for attractions along this stretch of road).

LBJ brought the attention of the world to his hometown, located 14 miles north from Blanco on US 281. Historic Johnson City was named for Sam Johnson, grandfather of President Lyndon Baines Johnson.

The most popular stop here is the LBJ Boyhood Home, managed by the U.S. Park Service. LBJ was five years old in 1913 when his family moved from their country home near the Pedernales River to this simple frame house. An adjacent Visitors Center provides information on this location, nearby Johnson Settlement, and other LBJ attractions. All are free of charge, a stipulation of the late president.

WHERE TO GO

Johnson Settlement. One block south of US 290 at Ninth St. Park at the Visitors Center, then walk to the Settlement for a look at the beginnings of the Johnson legacy. These rustic cabins and outbuildings once belonged to LBJ's grandfather, Sam Ealy Johnson, and his brother Tom. The two cattle drivers lived a rugged life in the hill country during the 1860s and '70s. An exhibit center tells this story in pictures and artifacts. You also can tour the brothers' cabins and see costumed docents carrying out 19th-century chores. Open daily. Free.

LBJ Boyhood Home. Next to the Johnson Settlement. LBJ was a schoolboy when his family moved here in 1913. The home is still furnished with the Johnsons' belongings. Guided tours are conducted every half hour. Open daily. Free.

WHERE TO EAT

Charles' Restaurant. US 281 as you enter town. If someone decided to make a poster of a typical Texas diner, they might choose Charles'. It's all here, from the Formica tables to the mirrored-glass pie display case. The chicken-fried steak holds up the Texas tradition. Open daily for breakfast, lunch, and dinner. $; []. (210) 868-4222.

STONEWALL

From Johnson City, head west on US 290 to the tiny community of Stonewall, the capital of the Texas peach industry. The road passes through miles of peach orchards, and during early summer, farm-fresh fruit is sold at roadside stands throughout the area. Stonewall is also the home of the LBJ National and State Historic Parks, encompassing the LBJ Ranch.

WHERE TO GO

LBJ National and State Historic Parks. Located west on US 290, these two combined parks together span approximately 700 acres. The area is composed of three main sections: the Visitors Center, the LBJ ranch and tour, and the Sauer-Beckman Farm. The most scenic route to the LBJ Park falls along RR 1, paralleling the wide, shallow Pedernales River. (Exit US 290 a few miles east of Stonewall.)

During Johnson's life, the ranch was closed to all but official visitors. In hopes of catching a glimpse of the president, travelers often stopped along RR 1, located across the river from the "Texas White House," the nickname of the Johnsons' home.

Today the parks draw visitors from around the world, who come for a look at the history behind the hill country, the presidency of LBJ, and a working Texas ranch.

Make your first stop the Visitors Center for a look at displays on LBJ's life, which include mementos of President Johnson's boyhood years. Attached to the Visitors Center is the Behrens Cabin, a dogtrot-style structure built by a German immigrant in the 1870s. Inside, the home is furnished with household items from over a century ago.

While you're in the Visitors Center, sign up for a free 90-minute guided tour of the LBJ Ranch, operated by the National Park Service. Tour buses run from 10 a.m. to 4 p.m. daily and travel across the President's ranch, making a stop at the one-room Junction School where Johnson began his education. Other stops include a look at the reconstructed birthplace home as well as the family cemetery where the former president is buried.

Near the end of the tour, the bus makes an optional stop at the Sauer-Beckman Living Historical Farm. The two 1918 farm homes are furnished in period style and manned by costumed interpreters who garden, tend livestock, and perform chores. Children can have a great time petting the farm animals. From here, it's just a short walk back to the Visitors Center.

Although the park does not have overnight facilities, there are two picnic areas and hiking trails for day use. Open daily. Free. (210) 644-2252 or 644-2241.

Grape Creek Vineyards. Four miles west of Stonewall on US 290. The fertile land of the Pedernales Valley is a natural for vineyards, and you'll find acres of beautiful grapevines at this winery that produces Cabernet Sauvignon and Chardonnay varieties. The winery is open Tuesday through Sunday from Easter through Labor Day, and Fridays and weekends in winter. Call for tour times. Free. (210) 644-2710.

LUCKENBACH

Waylon Jennings's popular country-western song made this community a Texas institution. The town consists of a shop or two and a small general store serving as a post office, dance hall, beer joint, and general gathering place.

To reach Luckenbach, leave Stonewall on US 290. Turn left on FM 1376 and continue for about 4¹/₄ miles. Don't expect to see signs pointing to the turnoff for Luckenbach Road; they were stolen as fast as the Highway Department could get them in the ground. After the turn for Grapetown, take the next right down a narrow country road. Luckenbach is just around the bend.

This town was founded in 1852 by Jacob, William, and August Luckenbach. The brothers opened a post office at the site and called it South Grape Creek. In 1886, a man named August Engel reopened the post office and renamed it Luckenbach in honor of the early founders.

The old post office is still there, the walls covered with scrawled names penned by Luckenbach fans. The store sells souvenirs of the town daily except Wednesdays. For more information on Luckenbach happenings, call (210) 997-3224.

FREDERICKSBURG

Retrace your steps from Luckenbach and continue west on US 290 to Fredericksburg, once the edge of the frontier and home to brave German pioneers. These first inhabitants faced many hardships, including hostile Comanche Indians; now the town is a favorite with antique shoppers, history buffs, and fans of good German food.

US 290 runs through the heart of the downtown district, becoming Main Street within the city limits. Originally the street was designed to be large enough to allow a wagon and team of mules to turn around in the center of town. Today, Main Street is filled with shoppers who come to explore the stores and restaurants of downtown Fredericksburg.

WHERE TO GO

Fredericksburg Chamber of Commerce. 112 W. Main St. Stop by the Chamber offices for brochures, maps, and information on a self-guided walking tour of historic downtown buildings, many of which now house shops and restaurants. The Chamber also can direct you to bed and breakfast facilities in the area. Open Monday through Saturday. Free. (210) 997-6523.

Admiral Nimitz State Historical Park. 340 E. Main St. This historic park is composed of three sections: the former Nimitz Steamboat Hotel, the Garden of Peace, and the Pacific History Walk.

Admiral Chester Nimitz, World War II Commander-in-Chief of the Pacific (CinCPac), was Fredericksburg's most famous resident. He commanded 2.5 million troops from the time he assumed command 18 days after the attack on Pearl Harbor until the Japanese surrendered.

The Nimitz name was well known here even years earlier. Having spent time in the merchant marines, the Admiral's grandfather, Captain Charles H. Nimitz, decided to build a hotel here, adding a structure much like a ship's bridge to the front of his establishment. Built in 1852, the Nimitz Steamboat Hotel catered to guests who enjoyed a room, a meal, and the use of an outdoor bathhouse.

Today the former hotel houses a three-story museum honoring Admiral Nimitz and Fredericksburg's early residents. Many exhibits are devoted to World War II, including several that illustrate the Pacific campaign. In addition to displays that record the building's past, several early hotel rooms, the hotel kitchen, and the bathhouse have been restored.

Behind the museum lies the Garden of Peace, a gift from the people of Japan. This classic Japanese garden includes a flowing stream, a raked bed of pebble and stones representing the sea and the Pacific islands, and a replica of the study used by Admiral Togo, Nimitz's counterpart in the Japanese forces.

Follow the signs from the Garden of Peace for one block to the Pacific History Walk. This takes you past a collection of military artifacts including a "fat man" Nagasaki-type atomic bomb case, a Japanese tank, and a restored barge like the one used by Nimitz. Open daily. Fee. (210) 997-4379.

Pioneer Museum Complex. 309 W. Main St. This collection of historic old homes includes a 1849 pioneer log home and store, the old First Methodist Church, and a smokehouse and log cabin. Also on the premises you'll see a typical 19th-century "Sunday house." Built in Fredericksburg, Sunday houses catered to farmers who would travel long distances to do business in town, often staying the weekend. With the advent of the automobile, such accommodations became obsolete. Today the old Sunday houses scattered throughout the town are used as bed and breakfasts, shops, and even private residences. They are easy to identify by their small size and the fact that most have half-story outside staircases. Call for hours. Fee. (210) 997-2835.

Bauer Toy Museum. 233 E. Main St. This museum houses over 3,000 antique toys dating from the late 19th century to the early mid-20th. Also on hand is a collection of old Texas license plates and a miniature replica of a small Texas town. Open Wednesday through Monday. Free. (210) 997-9394.

Pari-mutuel Horse Racing. At Gillespie County Fairgrounds on TX 16 South. From May through August, weekend quarterhorse races are held just outside of town. Fee. (210) 997-6523.

Fort Martin Scott. 1606 E. Main St., two miles east of Fredericksburg on US 290. Established in 1848, this was the first frontier military fort in Texas. Today the original stockade, a guardhouse, and a visitors center with displays on local Indians are open to tour, and historic reenactments keep the history lesson lively. Ongoing archaeological research conducted here offers a glimpse about the fort's past. Open Wednesday through Sunday from March to the end of the summer; Friday though Sunday the remainder of the year. Fee. (210) 997-9895.

Vereins Kirche Museum. Market Square on Main St. across from the Courthouse. You can't miss this attraction: it's housed in an exact replica of an octagonal structure erected in 1847. Back then the edifice was used as a church, as well as a school, fort, meeting hall, and storehouse.

The museum is sometimes called the Coffee Mill (or Die Kaffe-Muehle) Church because of its unusual shape. Exhibits here display Fredericksburg's German heritage, plus Indian artifacts from archaeological digs. Open Monday through Saturday from March through September, and Monday through Friday the rest of the year. Fee. (210) 997-7832 or 997-2835.

WHERE TO EAT

Altdorf German Biergarten and Restaurant. 301 W. Main St. Take a break from shopping and enjoy some good German food in a pleasant outdoor setting. Sandwiches, steaks, burgers, and Mexican food are served here as well. There's also dining in an adjacent stone building erected by the city's pioneers. The restaurant is open for lunch and dinner daily; closed February. $-$$; []. (210) 997-7774.

WHERE TO SHOP

Fredericksburg's many specialty shops offer antiques, linens, Texana, art, and collectibles. Most stores are housed in historic buildings along Main Street.

Charles Beckendorf Gallery. On US 290 just before entering Fredericksburg. This enormous gallery showcases the locally known work of artist Charles Beckendorf and is a good place to pick up a print of regional scenes, from one-room schoolhouses to brilliant fall scenics. Open daily. (210) 997-5955.

Hand Carved Candles. 121 E. Main St. and 155 E. Main St. Here artisans fashion unique hand-dipped and intricately carved candles. The larger of the stores, at 121 E. Main Street, has rooms filled with Christmas candles and ornaments of every description. You may find yourself with the holiday spirit even when the thermometer reads 100 degrees on an August afternoon. Open daily. (210) 997-2933 or 997-5259.

The Dulcimer Factory. 155 E. Main St. and 715 S. Washington St. The Washington Street factory carries hand-crafted folk instruments made from cherry, cypress, sassafras, birch, walnut, and maple woods. Free factory tours are given from 10 a.m. to 4 p.m. on weekdays. The Main Street retail store is open daily. (210) 997-6904 for information on the factory; (210) 997-2626 for the store.

Iron Art. 605 E. Main St. Many hill country ranches have metal signs over the entrance, often adorned with cut-out silhouettes of deer, cattle, or horses. Welder Dale Holly creates these works of art as well as wall hangings, wind chimes, weather vanes, and planters. Many of Holly's creations feature traditional Texas symbols such as the lone star and the Texas longhorn, as well as country designs like cats and pigs. Open daily. (210) 997-8307.

The Old Peanut Factory. 207 E. Park St., four blocks south of Main St. This old factory has been transformed into an arts and crafts marketplace, with some antiques and collectibles sprinkled in as well. The 15,000-square-foot building is filled with everything from Christmas ornaments to Texas T-shirts. Open daily. (210) 997-5008.

WHERE TO STAY

Best Western Sunday House Motel. 501 E. Main St. This 85-room family motel is within walking distance of shopping and the museums. $$; []. (800) 27-GERMAN or (210) 997-4484.

Gastehaus Schmidt. 231 W. Main St. This service represents 65 bed and breakfast accommodations, including cottages, log cabins, and a 125-year-old rock barn. All price ranges; []. (210) 997-5612.

ESPECIALLY FOR WINTER TEXANS

If you're traveling by RV or trailer, spend some time at the 113-site Lady Bird Johnson Municipal Park, just southwest of Fredericksburg on TX 16. Campsites have electrical, water, sewer, and cable TV hookups. There's a 14-day limit on camping from April through September.

The park also sports a nine-hole golf course, six tennis courts, and badminton and volleyball courts. There's also a 17-acre lake for fishing. For more information, call (210) 997-4202, or write: Lady Bird Municipal Park, P.O. Box 111, Fredericksburg, TX 78624.

ENCHANTED ROCK STATE PARK

Whether you're a climber or just looking for a good picnic spot, drive out to Enchanted Rock State Park. Located 18 miles north of Fredericksburg on RR 965, this state park features the largest stone formation in the West. Nationally this 640-acre granite outcropping takes second only to Georgia's Stone Mountain. According to Indian legend, the rock is haunted. Sometimes, when the rock cools at night, it makes a creaking sound, which probably accounts for the story.

People of all ages in reasonably good physical condition can enjoy a climb up Enchanted Rock. The walk takes about an hour, and hikers are rewarded with a magnificent view of the hill country. In warm weather (from April through October), start your ascent early in the morning before the relentless sun turns the rock into a griddle.

Experienced climbers can scale the smaller formations located adjacent to the main dome. These bare rocks are steep and dotted with boulders and crevices, and their ascent requires special equipment.

Picnic facilities and a 60-site primitive campground at the base of the rock round out the offerings here. No vehicular camping is permitted. Buy all your supplies in Fredericksburg; there are no concessions here. Open daily. Fee. (915) 247-3903.

Day Trip 1

AUSTIN

AUSTIN

San Antonio and Fort Worth have their colorful history, Dallas its corporate and financial image, and Houston its aerospace and shipping ties. But Austin has youth, vitality, and some outstanding attractions. Texas's fifth largest city, it boasts a population of 485,000 plus over 50,000 students at the University of Texas campus. There are at least an equal number of holdovers from the town's flower-child days of the 1960s and '70s. The result is an atmosphere of fun for the young and the young at heart.

Located 80 miles north from San Antonio on I-35, this capital city dates back to 1838, when Mirabeau B. Lamar, president-elect of the Texas Republic, came here to hunt buffalo. He found an even greater prize: a home for the new capital. Lamar fell in love with Waterloo, a tiny settlement surrounded by rolling hills and fed by cool springs. By the next year, the government had arrived and construction on the capitol building had begun.

Today's Austin straddles both sides of the Colorado River. Once unpredictable during rainy years, the Colorado has been tamed into a series of seven lakes, including two within Austin's city limits: Lake Austin and Town Lake.

Lake Austin begins at the foot of the hill country and flows for 22 miles through the western part of the city. Although high-priced residential structures are scattered along the shores, much of the countryside is still preserved in public parks.

Lake Austin empties into Town Lake, a narrow stretch of water that slices through the center of downtown. Beautifully planted greenbelts compose the shoreline, which also includes 15 miles of hike and bike trails. Although swimming and motorboating are prohibited, visitors can rent canoes near the lakeside Hyatt Regency hotel. The calm waters of Town Lake draw collegiate rowing teams from around the country to train in the warm climate.

Attractions abound on both sides of the Colorado River, most just a few minutes off I-35. A bit north of the river and within five minutes of the interstate are the best two shows in town: the Texas Legislature and the University of Texas. The legislature meets in the State Capitol from January through May in odd-numbered years. Even when this body is not in session, you can take a free tour of the historic building and watch the hustle and bustle of state government.

15

Parking in the capitol and downtown area is at a premium. The best way to explore is aboard a 'Dillo, the green trolley that starts at the Coliseum's free parking lot at the intersection of West Riverside Drive at Bouldin Avenue. The trolley travels up and down the streets from the river to the University.

From the capitol, it's a 10-minute walk north on Congress Avenue to Martin Luther King Boulevard and the southern edge of the University of Texas campus. This sprawling institution boasts students and faculty from around the world and some of the finest educational facilities in the country. The centerpiece of the university is the Main Tower, illuminated by orange lights whenever the University of Texas Longhorns win. The tower stands in the open mall, which includes the large Student Union building where students and the general public can grab a low-priced lunch.

Guadalupe (pronounced in Austin as "GWAD-a-loop") Street divides the educational campus from a commercial strip called "The Drag," the stretch of Guadalupe that runs from Martin Luther King Boulevard to 26th Street. The area is always crowded and fun, filled with shops and eateries that cater to every student need. The People's Renaissance Market, just across the street from the Student Union, is an open-air market where craftsmen sell their wares. It's especially popular with Austinites for Christmas shopping.

Most of the University of Texas campus is closed to motorized traffic, but you can park at the LBJ Presidential Library, located on the north side of campus. Before touring the Presidential Library, walk to the fountain for an unparalleled view of the campus and downtown Austin.

As your day draws to a close, head back to Town Lake. During summer months, people flock to the shoreline near the Congress Avenue Bridge to witness the nightly departure of thousands of bats from their home beneath the bridge. This is the largest Mexican free-tailed bat colony in a North American city. These mammals provide a very beneficial service by devouring millions of insects nightly. A kiosk containing information on the bat colony sits just behind the Four Seasons Hotel on the north shore of the lake.

Finally, spend your evening on Sixth Street, Austin's entertainment district that runs from Congress Avenue east to I-35. It's lined with restaurants, bars, and clubs featuring nightly music performed by Austin musicians. Friday and Saturday evenings are crowded. Be forewarned: Many clubs don't crank up the music until the wee hours.

WHERE TO GO

Visitor Information Center. 300 Bouldin Ave. Stop here for attractions, trolley and bus routes, and dining information. Open daily and Sunday afternoons. Free. (512) 478-0098.

State Capitol. 11th St. and Congress Ave. You might think that Texas's motto is "The bigger, the better," especially after a visit to the State Capitol. Taller than its national counterpart, the pink granite building houses the governor's office, the Texas Legislature, and several other executive state agencies.

Guided tours depart from the first floor rotunda from 8:30 a.m. to 4:30 p.m. daily. Free. (512) 463-0063.

Governor's Mansion. 1010 Colorado St. For over 130 years, Texas governors have enjoyed the opulence of this grand home. Visitors are taken past the main staircase, through the formal parlor, and finally into the dining room. Tours are conducted Monday through Friday. Call for hours; the home is sometimes closed because of incoming dignitaries. Free. (512) 463-5516.

LBJ Presidential Library. 2313 Red River St. From I-35, exit west at 26th St. Located on the campus of the University of Texas, this facility serves as a reminder of the hill country's most famous resident, Lyndon Baines Johnson. The library is filled with over 35 million historic documents, housed in archival boxes and available for scholarly research. The first two floors offer films on Johnson's life and career, as well as exhibits featuring jeweled gifts from foreign dignitaries and simpler handmade tokens from appreciative Americans. Visitors also can take in special displays of political, Civil Rights, and educational memorabilia. The top floor holds a reproduction of LBJ's White House Oval Office furnished as it was during his term. Open daily. Free. (512) 482-5279.

Zilker Park. From I-35, take the Riverside Dr. exit west and continue to Barton Springs Rd. Follow Barton Springs Rd. to the park. Located just south of Town Lake, this city park is a favorite with joggers, picnickers, swimmers, soccer teams, and kite flyers. Here lies the beautiful spring-fed Barton Springs pool, where you can take a dip in the 68-degree, crystal-clear waters all year. Things to see include a miniature train for the kids, a Japanese garden, a rose garden, and a nature center. Free; fee for pool and train. (512) 472-4914.

Town Lake Cruises. Depart from dock of Hyatt Regency Hotel at 208 Barton Springs Rd. Enjoy a 90-minute excursion on Town Lake aboard the *Lone Star* paddle wheeler. Call for schedule. Fee. (512) 327-1388.

Elisabet Ney Museum. 304 E. 44th St. German immigrant Elisabet Ney was considered Texas's first sculptress, and this stone building served as her studio and home. It's filled with her statues, working drawings, and personal belongings. Ney's work also can be seen in the entrance of the State Capitol. Open Wednesday through Sunday. Free. (512) 458-2255.

Laguna Gloria Art Museum. 3809 W. 35th St. This Mediterranean-style villa, located on Lake Austin, was built in 1916. Today the elegant structure is home to a museum that hosts changing exhibits of 20th-century art. Open Tuesday through Sunday. Fee; free on Thursday. (512) 458-8191.

National Wildflower Research Center. From Martin Luther King Blvd., drive east; the boulevard becomes Webberville Rd. after crossing US 183. Continue for four miles past the intersection of FM 973. Turn right at the light and drive for 1½ miles.

This unique institution is the only one in the nation devoted to the conservation and promotion of native plants and flowers. The center was the dream of Lady Bird Johnson, the wife of the late president. Mrs. Johnson is also responsible for the beautiful bluebonnet and wildflower plantings along the interstate highways in Texas.

Visitors can take a self-guided educational tour of the grounds; groups of 10 or more may arrange for a guide. The center acts as an information clearinghouse, distributing numerous fact sheets on the more than 100 native species. Annual events include landscaping seminars and workshops. The center is open Monday through Friday, with additional hours during the peak season of April and May. Free, although the center suggests a per car donation. (512) 929-3600.

WHERE TO EAT

Austin is filled with restaurants of every description, ranging from vegetarian to Vietnamese. For a list of Austin eateries, stop by the Austin Visitors Center at 300 Bouldin Avenue, located between Palmer Auditorium and City Auditorium. The Visitors Center is open seven days a week.

Sixth Street has many restaurants and bars featuring live music, especially blues. Most of the dining establishments are casual.

Trudy's Texas Star. 409 W. 30th St. This popular university-area restaurant feeds you Tex-Mex for breakfast, lunch, and dinner. The green chicken (meaning the sauce, not the chicken) enchiladas are the best in town. Open daily. $-$$; []. (512) 495-1867.

Foothills Grill. Hyatt Regency Austin, 208 Barton Springs Rd. This hotel restaurant is popular for its unbeatable view of the lake and the downtown highrise buildings. Specialties include sizzling fajitas and jumbo margaritas. $$; []. (512) 477-1234.

Iron Works Barbecue. 100 Red River St. This former foundry is still decorated with branding irons. Diners flock here to enjoy plates of juicy barbecue. If you have a big appetite, order the ribs. $-$$; []. (512) 478-4855.

Threadgill's. 6416 N. Lamar Blvd. Janis Joplin used to sing in this restaurant back in the early '60s. Today the place is best known for its home-style cooking, including jumbo chicken-fried steaks, fried chicken, and home-style vegetables like Grandma used to make. Open for breakfast, lunch, and dinner. $-$$; []. (512) 451-5440.

Chuy's. 1728 Barton Springs Rd. Chuy's takes great pride in being one of the strangest restaurants in town. With the name, you might expect Chinese food, but you'll get Tex-Mex in a funky decor featuring multitudes of those Elvis-on-black-velvet paintings. The food is great, but watch out for the spiciest dishes. They're ultra hot, even for seasoned Tex-Mex lovers. $; []. (512) 474-4452.

WHERE TO STAY

Hyatt Regency Austin. 208 Barton Springs Rd. This 448-room hotel has a signature Hyatt lobby, with glass elevators, a flowing stream, and a beautiful view of Town Lake. $$$; []. (512) 477-1234.

Four Seasons Hotel. 98 San Jacinto Blvd. Located on the northern edge of Town Lake, this hotel has a Southwestern atmosphere and a great view of the lake. Its back terrace is very popular with Austinites during the summer months, affording patrons one of the best looks at the city's famed Town Lake bat colony. $$$; []. (512) 478-4500.

Driskill Hotel. 112 E. Sixth St. Built in 1886 by cattle baron Jesse Driskill, this is Austin's oldest hotel. Its 177 rooms and beautiful lobby recall an elegant age in the city's history. The hotel sits within easy walking distance of the State Capitol and the Sixth Street entertainment district. Two restaurants and bars offer food and refreshment to guests preferring to "stay in." $$$; []. (800) 252-9367 or (512) 474-5911.

Day Trip 2
SAN MARCOS
BUDA

SAN MARCOS

San Marcos is located 51 miles northeast of San Antonio on I-35. It's a drive that's always busy, especially on Friday and Sunday afternoons.

Like neighboring New Braunfels, San Marcos is best known for its pure spring waters. The San Marcos River, which has been used by man for over 13,000 years, flows through town, providing the city with beautiful swimming and snorkeling spots and an amusement park.

Permanent settlement of the area began in 1845. Today San Marcos is a popular tourist town and the home of Southwest Texas State University.

WHERE TO GO

Tourist Information Center. Exit 206 (Aquarena Springs Dr.) from I-35 on the northwest side of town. Stop here for brochures on area attractions and accommodations, as well as free maps. Open daily. Free.

Aquarena Springs Resort. Take Aquarena Springs exit from I-35 and follow signs west of the highway. This resort dates back to 1928, when A. B. Rogers purchased 125 acres at the headwaters of the San Marcos River to create a grand hotel. He added glass-bottomed boats to cruise Spring Lake, fed by over 200 springs that produce 150 million gallons daily. This 98% pure water is home to many fish (including some white albino catfish) and various types of plant life.

Today visitors can still enjoy a cruise on the glass-bottomed boats and see the site of an underwater archaeological dig that unearthed the remains of Clovis Man, one of the hunter-gatherers who lived on the San Marcos River over 13,000 years ago.

Six rides and shows are all built on the theme of the river and its history. The park's mascot, Ralph the Swimming Pig, performs daily at the submarine theater, the only such theater in the world according to the park's owners. Attached to land at all times, the enclosed "submarine" viewing area submerges to take you below the crystalline waters of Spring Lake for the show.

The Alpine Sky Ride and the 300-foot-tall Sky Spiral offer a bird's-eye view of the park. From the Sky Spiral, you can see miles of beautiful rolling Texas hill country below.

Open daily, although hours change seasonally. Fee. (800) 999-9767 or (512) 396-8900.

Wonder World. Exit at Wonder World Dr. on south side of San Marcos and follow signs for about a mile.

A guided tour lasting nearly two hours covers the entire park, including the 7½-acre Texas Wildlife Park, Texas's largest petting zoo. A miniature train chugs through the animal enclosure, stopping to allow riders to pet and feed white-tail deer, wild turkeys, and many exotic species.

The next stop on the tour is Wonder Cave, created during a 3½-minute earthquake 30 million years ago. The same earthquake produced the Balcones Fault, an 1800-mile line separating the western hill country from the flat eastern farmland. Within the cave is the actual crack in the two land masses, containing huge boulders lodged in the fissure.

At the end of the cave tour, take the elevator ride to the top of the 110-foot Tejas Tower, which offers a spectacular view of the Balcones Fault and the contrasting terrain it produced.

The last stop is the Anti-Gravity House, a structure employing optical illusions and a slanted floor to create the feeling that you're leaning backwards. In this house, water appears to run "uphill," creating yet another illusion.

Open daily. Fee. (800) 782-7653, Ext. CAVE, or (512) 392-3760 for group and tour reservations.

A. E. Wood Fish Hatchery. Exit 204A from I-35; one mile south of San Marcos on FM 621. Large- and smallmouth bass and channel catfish are raised in this $14 million facility adjacent to the San Marcos River. Open Monday through Friday. Free. (512) 353-0572.

Historic Tours. Take a self-guided walking tour of downtown to San Marcos's earliest buildings, including the area's first cabin. A two-hour driving excursion takes you along part of the old Camino Real, or King's Highway. A brochure is available for a fee from the San Marcos Chamber of Commerce (800-782-7653, Ext. 177) or the Tourist Information Center at I-35 exit 206.

WHERE TO SHOP

San Marcos Factory Shops. Exit 200 from I-35 on the south side of San Marcos. This open-air mall features over 60 shops that sell direct from the factory. Luggage, shoes, leather goods, outdoor gear, china, and kitchen goods and other specialties are offered for sale. Chartered buses from as far as Dallas and Houston stop here regularly. Open daily. (512) 396-2200.

WHERE TO STAY

Aquarena Springs Inn. Located on the grounds of Aquarena Springs Resort, this hotel opened in 1928 as the Spring Lake Hotel. Today the refurbished inn offers many rooms with beautiful views of Spring Lake. The lake is no longer used for swimming because the aquatic life is so dense (some plants can grow up to six inches a day and must be "mowed" frequently). However, there is a large pool and a full-service restaurant. Room rates include a continental breakfast as well as a 50% discount on tickets to Aquarena Springs Resort and 50% off resort golfing. $$; []. (512) 396-8901.

BUDA

From San Marcos, it's an easy 15-minute drive north on I-35 to Buda, a former railroad town located on Loop 4 (Main Street) west of the highway.

Buda is one of the most mispronounced communities in Texas (and with names like Gruene, Leakey, and Boerne around, that's saying a lot). To sound like a local, just say "b-YOU-da." The name has caused more than one foreign visitor to come here expecting an old-world Hungarian settlement. Though possibly a reference to Budapest, it's more likely of Spanish origin.

According to legend, several widows cooked in the local hotel restaurant that was popular with employees of the International-Great Northern Railroad. The Spanish word for widow is *viuda*. Since the "v" is pronounced as a "b" in Spanish, Buda may be a phonetic spelling for viuda.

Buda is still a railroad town, with double tracks running parallel to Main Street.

WHERE TO SHOP

Many Buda stores are closed Monday through Wednesday, although some are open by appointment. Most shops are located in a two-block stretch of Main Street.

BW's Boutique. Main St. This arts and crafts shop, owned by the Buda Women's Club, features everything from watercolors to locally made furniture. Open Wednesday through Sunday. (512) 295-3373.

Don's Den. Main St. This antique shop has a little of everything, but it specializes in toys, electric trains, and metal cars. Open Wednesday through Sunday. (512) 295-5211.

Memory Lane Antiques. Main St. This two-story shop has a good selection of quilts, collectibles, and refinished furniture. Open daily. (512) 295-2434.

Texas Hatters. Exit 220 on east side of I-35. Owner Manny Gammage could be called "Texas's hatmaker to the stars." His hats have topped the heads of Roy Rogers, Willie Nelson, Ronald Reagan, Burt Reynolds, and many other celebrities whose pictures decorate the shop walls. Besides the obligatory cowboy hats, this store also sells hand-blocked hi-rollers, Panamas, and derbies. Gammage also offers hatbands, many of which are handmade by the weaver in the adjoining store. Open Tuesday through Saturday. (512) 295-HATS or 441-HATS.

Day Trip 3
NEW BRAUNFELS
GRUENE

NEW BRAUNFELS

If you're looking for a romantic getaway in a historic inn or a weekend of outdoor fun, New Braunfels is the place. Just half an hour northeast of San Antonio on I-35, this town of 25,000 offers something for every interest, from antiques and water sports to German culture.

In the 1840s, a group of German businessmen bought some land in Texas, planning to parcel off the acreage to German immigrants. Led by Prince Carl of Germany's Solms-Braunfels region, the group came to Texas to check on their new purchase. They discovered that it was over 300 miles from the Texas coast, far from supplies in San Antonio and located in the midst of Comanche Indian territory.

Prince Carl sent a letter warning other settlers not to come, but it was too late—almost 400 already had set sail for Texas. The prince saved the day by buying another parcel of land, this in the central part of the state. Called "The Fountains" by the Indians, it offered plentiful springs and agricultural opportunities. The Germans soon divided the land into farms, irrigating with spring water. The settlement they founded was named New Braunfels in honor of their homeland.

New Braunfels has never forgotten these ties to the old country. Even today, German is spoken in many local homes. Every November the town puts on its lederhosen for Wurstfest, one of the largest German celebrations in the country.

The German settlers were a practical lot, and they saved old items of every description. Everything from handmade cradles to used bottles and jars were kept and passed down through generations. Because of this, New Braunfels touts itself as "The Antique Capital of Texas."

The early settlers of New Braunfels also were attracted by the Comal and Guadalupe Rivers. Today swimmers, rafters, inner-tubers, and campers are drawn to these shady banks. The two-mile long Comal holds the distinction as the world's shortest river. Its crystal clear waters begin with the springs in downtown Landa Park, eventually merging with the Guadalupe River, home to many local outfitters. Located on the scenic drive called River Road, the outfitters provide equipment and transportation for inner-tubers and rafters of all skill levels who like nothing better on a hot Texas day than to float down the cypress-shaded waters.

WHERE TO GO

Chamber of Commerce. 390 S. Seguin Ave. Drop by for maps, brochures, shopping information, and friendly hometown advice about the area. Open Monday through Friday. (800) 572-2626.

Schlitterbahn. 305 W. Austin St. From I-35, take the Boerne exit (Loop 337) to Common St. Take a left and continue to Liberty St. This water park ranks first in Texas and fourth in the United States in number of visitors. With 65 acres, this is the largest water theme park in the state.

Schlitterbahn, which means "slippery road" in German, is also the largest tubing park in the world, with nine man-made chutes. The Comal River supplies 24,000 gallons a minute of cool spring water and also provides the only natural river rapids found in a water theme park.

Among the most colorful rides are the "Soda Straws," huge plexiglass enclosed slides that take riders from the top of a 27-foot concrete soda to a pool below. In 1986 the cola glasses were filled with 2,000 gallons of soda and Blue Bell ice cream to create the world's largest Coke float.

There's a steep 60-foot Schlittercoaster and the mile-long Raging River tube chute for daredevils, and a 50,000 gallon hot tub with a swim-up bar and the gentle wave pool for the less adventurous.

Plan to spend a whole day here, and bring a picnic if you like. Open May through September. Fee. (210) 625-2351.

Hummel Museum. 199 Main Plaza. This 15,000-square-foot collection is the newest attraction in town. The museum chronicles the life of German nun Sister Maria Innocentia Hummel through her sketches, paintings, and personal diaries. It's filled with 350 original paintings and early sketches that spawned the popular Hummel figurines, plates, and other collectibles. Sister Maria Innocentia first began producing these works during World War II. Today the figurines and plates, which portray young children, are sought by collectors from around the world. Occasionally the museum brings craftsmen from Germany to demonstrate the production of today's Hummel items. Collectors will find a Hummel bonanza in the adjacent gift shop. Fee. (210) 456-4866.

Sophienburg Museum. 401 W. Coll St. For a look at the hard-working people who settled this rugged area, spend an hour or two at the Sophienburg. Named for the wife of settlement leader Prince Carl, the museum's displays include a reproduction of an early New Braunfels home, a doctor's office (complete with medical tools), a blacksmith's shop, and carriages used by early residents. Open daily, but call for hours. Fee. (210) 629-1572.

Lindheimer Home. 491 Comal Ave. Located on the banks of the Comal River, this home belonged to Ferdinand Lindheimer, a botanist who lent his name to over 30 Texas plant species. Now restored, it contains early memorabilia from Lindheimer's career as both botanist and newspaper publisher. A backyard garden is filled with examples of his native flora discoveries. Hours are seasonal; call before you go. Fee. (210) 625-8766.

Museum of Texas Handmade Furniture. 1370 Church Hill Dr., in Conservation Plaza. This 19th-century home contains cedar, oak, and cypress furniture hand-crafted by early German settlers. Open Tuesday through Sunday from Memorial Day through Labor Day, and on weekend afternoons the rest of the year. Fee. (210) 629-6504.

Natural Bridge Caverns. On RR 3009, southwest of New Braunfels. Named for the rock arch over the entrance, this cave is one of the most spectacular in the area. The guided tour is well lit; the slope of the trail may be taxing for some. The cave is open year-round; phone for tour times. Open daily. Fee. (210) 651-6101.

Natural Bridge Wildlife Ranch. Next to the caverns. From I-35 south of New Braunfels, take RR 3009 west. From TX 46 west of town, you also can take a left on RR 1863 for a slightly longer but very scenic route. The drive through the ranch takes you past zebras, gazelles, antelopes, and ostriches, and feeding is allowed. The entrance area includes a petting zoo with pygmy goats. Open daily. Fee. (210) 438-7400.

Wildlife Wilderness. FM 306 exit off I-35 north of New Braunfels, west for seven miles. Like Natural Bridge, this ranch features exotic and local wildlife, but Wildlife Wilderness does not permit feeding on the drive. The petting area contains a friendly emu and Texas white-tail deer. Open daily; weekends only in January and February. Fee. (210) 964-3388.

Landa Park. Landa and San Antonio Sts. Named for Joseph Landa, New Braunfels's first millionaire, this downtown park includes a miniature train, a glass-bottomed boat cruise, a golf course, and a 1½-acre spring-fed swimming pool. This is the headwaters of the Comal River, where springs gush eight million gallons of pure water every hour. Picnicking is welcome in the park, but no camping. Free. (210) 625-3139.

Canyon Lake. FM 306, northwest of town. With 80 miles of protected shoreline, Canyon Lake is very popular with campers, cyclists, scuba divers, and boaters. The lake has seven parks with boat ramps and picnic facilities. (210) 964-2223.

River Road. This winding drive stretches northwest of the city for 15 miles from Loop 337 at the city limits to the Canyon Lake Dam. It's lined with river outfitters and beautiful spots to pull over and enjoy a look at the rapids, which delight rafters, canoeists, and inner-tubers alike.

WHERE TO SHOP

Antique Barn. Off I-35 at Seguin St. This tin building contains antiques of every description. The owners frequently buy the contents and fixtures of closed businesses, often ending up with old merchandise in original containers. The Antique Barn specializes in signs and Coca-Cola memorabilia. Open daily. (210) 620-1715.

New Braunfels Downtowner Antiques Mall. 223 W. San Antonio St., off the Plaza. This antique mall, spanning over 7,000 square feet, is filled with everything from Raggedy Ann dolls to old matchbooks. Closed Tuesday. (210) 629-3947.

Opa's Haus. 1600 River Rd., one-half mile north of Loop 337. Opa's Haus operates a secondary or resale market for limited edition collectibles. The store sells plates, steins, ornaments, and cuckoo clocks, as well as Hummel figurines. Open daily. (210) 629-1191.

Mill Store Plaza. Exits 187 and 189 off I-35. What started out as a factory store for West Point Pepperell has become a destination for busloads of shoppers from Houston and Dallas. The stores, which often sell new product lines, are owned by the factories, but unlike some factory outlets this mall does not feature second or discounted merchandise. Open daily. (210) 620-6806.

WHERE TO EAT

Langston House. 190 S. Seguin Ave. You wouldn't expect to find fine Continental dining in a small town, but that's what makes this restaurant so special. Owner Bill Knight is a former theater professional and has decorated the interior of the 1854 home with billboards and theater memorabilia. He also entertains diners with show tunes at the grand piano. The menu changes frequently. $$-$$$; []. (210) 625-1898.

Oma's Haus. Take Seguin exit off I-35 and drive east to 541 TX 46 south. This restaurant serves a wide selection of German dishes in a family atmosphere. The menu includes chicken and pork schnitzel, and a specialty of the house called Oma's Pride, a spinach-filled pastry shell. For the less adventurous, chicken-fried steak and chicken breast also are offered. Open for lunch and dinner daily. $$; []. (210) 625-3280.

Bavarian Village. 212 W. Austin St. Dine in the first two-story house in New Braunfels—the restaurant offers a long list of German delicacies. Behind the eatery, small shops sell specialty items including family crests and baked goods. The best part of the Bavarian Village is the biergarten, where polka dances are held every Saturday night and German bands entertain regulars and visitors alike. The "Chicken Dance" is a favorite here and at German festivals. If you're hungry, order the six-foot submarine sandwich or a 13-inch boiled egg shaped like a sausage. Open for lunch and dinner. $$-$$$; []. (210) 625-0815.

WHERE TO STAY

New Braunfels has plenty of accommodations for everyone. Check with the Chamber of Commerce (800-572-2626) or call Central Reservations (800-545-6606).

Prince Solms Inn. 295 E. San Antonio St. Built in 1900, this quiet bed and breakfast has two suites and a guest parlor downstairs; upstairs there are eight guest rooms. All rooms are furnished with period antiques. $$; []. (210) 625-9169.

Faust Hotel. 240 S. Seguin St. A New Braunfels tradition, this 1929 four-story, renovated hotel features a bar that's popular with locals and visitors. The lobby is appointed with beautiful antique furnishings. $$; []. (210) 625-7791.

ESPECIALLY FOR WINTER TEXANS

Heidelberg Lodges. 1020 N. Houston Ave. Located near the headwaters of the Comal River, this scenic family resort is popular in the summer with swimmers, snorkelers, and scuba divers. During off-season it's home to winter Texans, who are welcomed with potluck dinners and get-togethers. Accommodations include A-frame cottages and motel units. Call for long-term winter rates. $$; []. (210) 625-9967.

GRUENE

Gruene (pronounced "green") is located north of New Braunfels on Gruene Street just off Loop 337.

In the days when cotton was king, Gruene was a roaring town on the banks of the Guadalupe River. Started in the 1870s by H. D. Gruene, the community featured a swinging dance hall and a cotton gin. Prosperity reigned until the Great Depression came to Texas, with the boll weevil right on its heels. Gruene's foreman hanged himself from the water tower, and H. D.'s plans for the town withered like the cotton in the fields. Gruene became a ghost town.

One hundred years after its founding, investors began restoring Gruene's historic buildings and, little by little, businesses began moving into the once-deserted structures. Now Gruene is favored by antique shoppers, barbecue and country music lovers, and those looking to step back into a simpler time. On weekdays you may find Gruene's streets quiet, but expect crowds every weekend.

There's free parking across from the Gruene Mansion, former home of H. D. Gruene. Today the mansion is a private residence owned by the proprietors of an adjacent bed and breakfast.

Gruene is compact, with everything within easy walking distance. If you'd like more information on the community's history, pick up a free copy of "A Pedestrian Guide for Gruene Guests" at local shops. Paula Crow, owner of Texas Homegrown at 1641 Hunter Road, also provides walking tours. Call (210) 629-3176 to set one up.

Over 100 antique vendors sell their wares during Market Days. This event is held March through October on the third Saturday and Sunday of the month.

WHERE TO GO

Guadalupe Valley Winery. 1720 Hunter Rd. Housed in an old cotton gin, this winery produces excellent wines made from grapes grown throughout the state. Step up to the bar for a free sample of their product. Tours are given on the third weekend of the month, March through October. The tasting room is open daily. Free. (210) 629-2351.

Texas Wines. 1612 Hunter Rd. This shop serves as a tasting room and a distributor for many Texas wine makers. Free. (210) 620-4503.

Gruene Hall. 1281 Gruene Rd. The oldest dance hall in Texas is as lively today as it was a century ago. Dances and concerts are often held here (even though the hall still offers only natural air conditioning), and it is also open to tour. Burlap bags draped from the ceiling dampen the sound, 1930s advertisements decorate the walls, and a U.S. flag with 49 stars still hangs over the dance floor. Call for a schedule of events. (210) 625-0142.

WHERE TO SHOP

Bushwackers. 1633 Hunter Rd. Handmade swings hang beneath this store's shady oak trees. Craftsmen here produce outdoor furniture of all types as well as custom-made cypress and mesquite furniture. Open daily. (800) 676-4534 or (210) 620-4534.

Texas Homegrown. 1641 Hunter Rd. Like the name suggests, the merchandise here is Texas-themed and features everything from bluebonnet earrings to coyote T-shirts. Open daily; closed January. (210) 629-3176.

Gruene Antique Company. 1607 Hunter Rd. Built in 1904, this was once a general store. Today it's divided into several vendor areas and filled with antiques. Open daily. (210) 629-7781.

Buck Pottery. 1296 Gruene Rd. Here you can watch craftsmen make pottery in the back room. This shop sells dinnerware, gift items, and outdoor pots, all made with unleaded glazes. Open daily. (210) 629-7975.

Gruene Haus. 1297 Gruene Rd. Built in the 1880s, this shop was the former home of H. D. Gruene's foreman. Linens, lace runners, silk bluebonnets, gifts for cat lovers, and decorative accessories are offered for sale. Call owner Virginia Hughes for a tour of the backyard herb garden. Open daily. (210) 629-5990.

WHERE TO EAT

Guadalupe Smoked Meats. 1299 Gruene Rd. Outstanding barbecue, potato salad, and beans are popular choices at this restaurant. You can dine on an outdoor deck above the banks of the Guadalupe River. The owners also operate a mail-order business, for people who can't find barbecue like this at home. Open daily for lunch and dinner. $$; []. (210) 629-6121.

Grist Mill Restaurant. 1287 Gruene Rd. Housed in the ruins of a 100-year-old cotton gin, this restaurant serves fried chicken, chicken-fried steak, and other Texas favorites. You can eat inside or outside on the deck. Open daily for lunch and dinner; closed January. $$; []. (210) 625-0684.

WHERE TO STAY

Gruene Mansion Inn. 1275 Hunter Rd. This grand Victorian mansion was originally the home of H. D. Gruene. The inn overlooks the Guadalupe River and features eight lovely rooms decorated with period antiques. $$; no []. (210) 629-2641.

Day Trip 1
LULING
HARWOOD
FLATONIA
PRAHA
ENGLE
SCHULENBURG

LULING

You can leave San Antonio on either I-10 or US 90, traveling east past Seguin on your way to Luling. (For Seguin attractions, see EAST FROM SAN ANTONIO, DAY TRIP 2.)

Luling is best known as an oil town. Oil was discovered here in 1922 and fields pumping this "black gold" can be seen throughout the Luling area. Even before that time the town had a reputation as "the toughest town in Texas," frequented by gunfighters like John Wesley Hardin and Ben Thompson. Luling was also a cattle center and the end of a railroad line to Chihuahua, Mexico.

When oil was discovered, the economy of the town shifted to this profitable industry. Today 184 wells pump within the city limits. As part of a beautification effort, the Chamber of Commerce commissioned an artist to transform several of the pumpjacks into moving sculptures in the shapes of cartoon characters. There's even a Santa Claus, and a butterfly to brighten up the streets.

WHERE TO GO

Palmetto State Park. Six miles southeast of town on US 183, along the banks of the San Marcos River. Palmetto State Park is a topographical anomaly amidst gently rolling farm and ranchland. According to scientists, the river shifted course thousands of years ago, leaving a huge deposit of silt. This sediment absorbed rain and ground water, nurturing a marshy swamp estimated to be over 18,000 years old. Now part of Palmetto State Park, the swamp is filled with palmettos as well as moss-draped trees, four-foot-tall irises, and many bird species. Nature trails wind throughout the area.

The park has full hookups and tent sites. There's also picnicking, but during the warmer months bring along mosquito repellent. Open daily. Fee. (210) 672-3266.

HARWOOD

WHERE TO GO

Noah's Ark. TX 304, 5½ miles north of I-10, outside of Harwood. This drive-through exotic wildlife park boasts 500 animals. The 400-acre park is divided into 10 sanctuaries, covering animals of the plains and the mountains.

On your trip through the park, you can feed axis deer, Corsican sheep, red kangaroos, emus, camels, rhinos, and local favorites like Texas longhorns. A large petting area is home to Angora and pygmy goats, Sicilian donkeys, and more. A bird aviary contains exotic chickens, peacocks, and pheasants. Open daily except Christmas. Fee. (512) 540-4664.

FLATONIA

Return to US 90 and continue east to the small town of Flatonia. This community was settled by the English, German, Bohemian, and Czech immigrants, many of whom came to the United States in the 1850s and 1860s to avoid Austro-Hungarian oppression.

WHERE TO GO

Arnim Museum. US 90, downtown. This local history museum contains exhibits on Flatonia's early days and its settlement by many cultural groups. Open Sunday afternoon. Free. (512) 865-2451.

PRAHA

Three miles east of Flatonia on US 90 is Praha (the Slovakian spelling for "Prague"). Like its European counterpart, Praha holds a predominantly Czech population, descendants of immigrants who came here in 1855.

The main structure in Praha is the Assumption of the Blessed Virgin Mary Church, often called St. Mary's. Built in 1895, it is one of a half dozen painted churches in the area. Although few examples of these churches remain today, it was not unusual for 19th-century rural churches to boast painted interiors. Guided tours from nearby Schulenburg visit all the churches, but you can see most of the structures on a self-guided trip. A free brochure and map of these structures is available from the Schulenburg Chamber of Commerce (409-743-4514).

St. Mary's has a beautifully painted vaulted ceiling, the work of Swiss-born artist Gottfried Flury. Never retouched, the 1895 murals on the tongue-and-groove ceiling depict golden angels high over a pastoral setting. This Praha church, as well as ones in High Hill and Ammannsville, is listed in the National Register of Historic Places.

The Praha church is open to visitors. Free.

ENGLE

WHERE TO GO

Chudej's Place. North side of US 90 in Engle. Chudej's Place is the center of activity in town. Built in the 1800s, this old-fashioned bar's unpainted interior holds old advertisements pinned to the walls. Most of the locals who come here speak with a heavy Czech accent and are descended from those early settlers. Closed Tuesday.

SCHULENBURG

Continue east on US 90 to the agricultural community of Schulenburg (meaning "school town" in German). Carnation Milk Company's first plant was built in Schulenburg in 1929, and even today dairy products generate a major source of income for the area.

Schulenburg is known as the "Home of the Painted Churches," although the elaborately painted structures are actually located in nearby small communities (Dubina, Ammannsville, Swiss Alp, High Hill, and Praha). These beautifully painted buildings are reminders of the area's rural traditions and ethnic background.

In Ammannsville, the St. John the Baptist Church includes stained glass windows illustrating the Czech heritage of the parish. High Hill's St. Mary's Church boasts marbleized columns, religious statuary, and a history of a European-style seating arrangement with women on the left and men on the right.

The murals in Dubina's Sts. Cyril and Methodius Church were covered over during a 1952 remodeling. In 1981 the paintings, depicting winged angels and elaborate stencil patterns, were renovated by a local parishioner.

WHERE TO GO

Painted Churches Tour. With a two- to three-week notice, the Schulenburg Chamber of Commerce provides guides for groups of 15 or more. You can also obtain a free map of the church sites for a self-guided trip. Fee for guided tour only. (409) 743-4514.

Day Trip 2

SEGUIN
GONZALES
SHINER
YOAKUM

SEGUIN

You can reach Seguin (pronounced "se-GEEN") via either US 90 or I-10 east of San Antonio. It's a 36-mile trip to this town on the Guadalupe River, named for Lieutenant Colonel Juan Seguin, a hero of the Texas Revolution. Prior to the Mexican invasion of 1837, Seguin was ordered by his superiors to destroy San Antonio. He refused, thus saving the city.

Many towns boast nicknames, from Austin's "River City" to San Antonio's "Alamo City." Seguin, though, has one of the most unusual: "The Mother of Concrete Cities." A Seguin chemist held several concrete production patents, which accounts for the use of the material in over 90 area buildings by the end of the 19th century.

The most beautiful part of Seguin is Starke Park. It offers picnic tables under huge pecan, oak, and cypress trees, and a winding drive along the Guadalupe River.

WHERE TO GO

Chamber of Commerce. 427 N. Austin St. Stop by the Chamber office for brochures and maps. Open weekdays. (210) 379-6382.

Sebastapol State Historical Park. 704 Zorn St. This is one of the best examples of the early use of concrete in the Southwest. Sebastapol was once a large home, constructed of concrete with a plaster overlay. Today it is open for tours and contains exhibits illustrating the construction of this historic building and its restoration in 1988. Tours are conducted from Wednesday through Sunday. Fee. (210) 379-4833.

Starke Park. South side of town, off TX 123. Make time for this pleasant park, which offers golf, tennis, and baseball as well as many riverside picnic spots. Free. (210) 379-3212.

Seguin's Lakes. Seguin is surrounded by four lakes on the Guadalupe River that offer bass, crappie, and catfish fishing, including lighted docks for night fishing. RV facilities are available as well. The lakes include **Lake Dunlap**— I-10 to TX 46 exit west of Seguin, then eight miles on TX 46; **Lake McQueeney** —I-10 to FM 78 exit, FM 78 west for three miles to FM 725, then turn right and continue for one mile; **Lake Placid**—I-10 to FM 464 exit, stay on access road; and **Meadow Lake**—I-10 to TX 123 bypass, then south for four miles.

GONZALES

Take alternate US 90 (US 90A) east to Gonzales, one of Texas's most interesting historic cities. For many years this was the westernmost settlement in the state.

Plagued by constant Indian attacks, Gonzales's citizens received a small brass cannon for protection by the Mexican government in 1831. Four years later, when relations between Texas and Mexico soured, over 150 Mexican soldiers staged a battle to retrieve the weapon.

The soldiers were faced with 18 Gonzaleans, who stalled the army while local citizens rolled out the small field-piece and prepared for action. Meanwhile, other townsfolk sewed the first battle flag of Texas, which pictured a cannon beneath the words "Come and Take It," a motto by which Gonzales is still known. The Texans fired the first shot and the Mexican troops retreated. Although the confrontation was brief, this act began the Texas Revolution.

The site of this historic first conflict is marked by a monument located seven miles southwest of Gonzales on TX 97. The first shots were fired one-half mile north of the present monument.

WHERE TO GO

Chamber of Commerce. 414 St. Lawrence St. Located in the Old Jail, this office has brochures on local attractions and events. (210) 672-6532.

Old Jail Museum. 414 St. Lawrence St. This fascinating museum is housed in the old Gonzales jail, built in 1887 and used until 1975. Downstairs you can tour the room where female prisoners and mentally ill persons once were incarcerated together.

The walls of the second floor are chiseled with graffiti of past residents. The large room is rimmed with iron cells, all overlooking a reproduction of the old gallows that carried off its last hanging in 1921. The museum is open daily (afternoons only on Sunday.) Free. (210) 672-6532 (Chamber of Commerce).

Memorial Museum. 414 Smith St., between St. Lawrence and St. Louis Sts. This museum is dedicated to the history of Gonzales. Exhibits on the town's early days include the "Come and Take It" cannon. Open Tuesday through Sunday. Free. (210) 672-6350.

Gonzales Pioneer Village. One-half mile north of town on US 183. This living history center takes visitors back to Gonzales's frontier days. The village is composed of log cabins, a cypress-constructed home, a grand Victorian home, a smokehouse, a blacksmith shop, and a church. Tours are conducted by costumed interpreters. The village also stages reenactments, including the "Come and Take It" Celebration in October. Open Wednesday through Sunday. Fee. (210) 672-2157.

SHINER

Continue east on US 90A for 18 miles to Shiner, best known as the home of Shiner beer, a Texas favorite produced by the tiny Spoetzl Brewery since 1909.

WHERE TO GO

Spoetzl Brewery. 603 Brewery St., off TX 95 north. This tiny but historic brewery was founded in 1909 by Kosmos Spoetzl, a Bavarian brewmaster. Here Shiner and Shiner Bock beers are produced in one of the smallest brew kettles in the country. Across the street, a museum and gift shop overflow with Shiner memorabilia, antiques, and photos of Spoetzl's early days.

Free brewery tours at 11 a.m. on Monday through Thursday. Hospitality room open during working hours Monday through Friday; closed for lunch. Free. (512) 594-3852.

City Hall. US 90A downtown. This two-story building houses the fire department, police department, and city offices. Enter on the left side for city brochures and a free map. (512) 594-4180.

Guided Tours of Shiner. On the first and third Friday of each month, tours start at the brewery and stop at historic sites throughout town. Call for reservations. Fee. (512) 594-4343 or 594-4180.

YOAKUM

From Shiner, drive south on TX 95 for eight miles to US 77A. Turn right and continue for two miles.

Yoakum was the starting point of many cattle drives along the Chisholm Trail, and in 1887 it became the junction for the San Antonio and Aransas Pass Railroad. When the railroad came to town, meat packinghouses followed. In 1919 the first tannery opened, producing leather kneepads for cotton pickers. Soon more leather businesses arrived, and eventually Yoakum earned its title as "The Leather Capital of the World."

Today 11 leather companies produce belts, saddles, bullwhips, gunslings, and wallets. Although the companies do not sell directly from their factories, the

Leather Capital Store operates as a showroom and factory outlet for many Yoakum manufacturers.

Call the Chamber of Commerce at (512) 293-2309 to arrange a guided tour of a leather factory. Tours are usually stopped prior to Christmas season during peak production.

WHERE TO GO

Yoakum Heritage Museum. 312 Simpson St. This two-story museum is filled with Yoakum memorabilia, from railroad paraphernalia to household items. The most interesting exhibit area is the Leather Room, with its displays on the leather factories. Open afternoons daily. Free. (512) 293-7022.

WHERE TO SHOP

The Leather Capital Store. 123 W. Grand St. This shop is a leather museum and store rolled into one. Its display windows are painted with silhouettes of Texas history scenes. Inside, thousands of belts, purses, and boots—even gunslings and holsters—are offered for sale. Upstairs, the facade of a Wild West village brightens a floor filled with saddles and Southwestern and Western art. Deer shoulder blades etched with Indian scenes are produced by owner Leo Smith, who for many years worked as a commercial illustrator for one of the leather companies. Open Monday through Saturday. (512) 293-7274.

Return home from Yoakum by retracing your steps or by heading north on TX 95 to Flatonia. From here, go west on either I-10 or US 90. Attractions on this stretch are covered in EAST FROM SAN ANTONIO, DAY TRIP 1.

Day Trip 1

PANNA MARIA
GOLIAD

PANNA MARIA

To reach Panna Maria, leave San Antonio southeast on US 87. At the intersection of TX 123, drive south past the tiny Polish communities of Kosciusko and Cestohowa. At the intersection of FM 81, turn left for the one-mile drive to Panna Maria.

Although there's not much to see, this tiny community has an interesting history. It was founded in 1854 by 100 Polish families who came to central Texas on foot after arriving in Galveston. After surviving many hardships, they settled in the area and built the first Polish church and school in the country. Today Panna Maria is still populated by many families who speak Polish in their homes.

WHAT TO SEE

Church of the Immaculate Conception. TX 81, in town. Within two years of settling in Panna Maria, the pioneers built the Church of the Immaculate Conception, the first Polish church in America. The original church was destroyed by fire and replaced in 1878 by the present structure, which serves as the place of worship for Panna Maria's citizens.

The church is home to a replica of the mosaic of Our Lady of Czestochowa, or the Black Madonna. The original Black Madonna is enshrined at the Monastery of Jasna Gora in Czestochowa, Poland, a city about 65 miles east of the area from which the original Panna Maria pioneers originated. According to tradition, the Madonna was painted by St. Luke, and then found in the Holy Land in 326 by Saint Helena, mother of Constantine the Great.

This replica, a gift to the United States from Poland, was presented to the town by President Johnson in 1966. It is on display at the front of the church along with hand-carved chairs and a gold chalice that belonged to Pope John Paul II. These priceless treasures were presented to the people of Panna Maria in 1987.

The church is open daily. For a small donation, you can purchase a brochure outlining the history of the Black Madonna and Panna Maria's early settlers. Free. (210) 226-8381.

GOLIAD

To reach Goliad, continue southeast from Panna Maria on FM 81 past the communities of Helena and Runge, both of which were once thriving towns. Take TX 239 south at Charco to the intersection of US 59, and then head east to the historic city of Goliad.

Like the Alamo and the Battle of San Jacinto, Goliad holds a special place in Texas history. Founded by the Spanish, Goliad is the third oldest city in Texas. To protect their passage to the Gulf, the Spaniards moved their Espíritu Santo mission and its royal protector, Presidio La Bahia (Fort of the Bay), to this location in 1749. At that time the community was named Santa Dorotea. Years later, the town's name was changed to Goliad, an anagram of the spoken letters "Hidalgo" (the "h" is silent in Spanish). Hidalgo was a priest who became a hero during the Mexican Revolution.

Few towns have their own flag, but Goliad boasts its own historic, if somewhat gruesome, banner. On October 9, 1835, the Texas colonists made a move in their battle for independence. The settlers took over the Presidio and raised the "Bloody Arm Flag," picturing a severed arm holding a sword.

The next year the Texans, led by Colonel James Fannin, surrendered at the Battle of Coleto about nine miles east of town. Approximately 390 soldiers were marched back to the Presidio. After a week of imprisonment all but 20 soldiers (who were spared as physicians or mechanics) were placed before a firing squad. Over two dozen men escaped during the massacre, but 342 were killed, the largest loss of life during the fight for independence. "Remember Goliad" soon became a cry alongside "Remember the Alamo."

Today the Presidio and the Mission Espíritu Santo are restored and open to the public. You also can visit Colonel Fannin's grave and see the monument that marks the resting place of the Texas soldiers.

WHAT TO SEE

Goliad State Historical Park. On US 183, one-fourth mile south of town. The highlight of this 178-acre park is the Mission Espíritu Santo. The restored mission offers spinning, weaving, and pottery-making demonstrations, primarily on weekends. Park activities feature hiking, picnicking, fishing, and boating. Screened shelters as well as tent and RV camping sites are available year-round. Fee. (512) 645-3405.

Presidio La Bahia. US 183 south of the San Antonio River. The Presidio holds many titles: It is the oldest fort in the West, one of few sites west of the Mississippi that was active in the American Revolution, the only fully restored Spanish Presidio, and the only Texas Revolutionary site with its original appearance intact. The stone garrison is impressive and worth a stop. While you're here, visit the fort chapel, built in the Spanish colonial style. Open daily. Fee. (512) 645-3752.

General Zaragoza Birthplace. Across from the Presidio La Bahia. This modest structure was the first home of Mexican General Ignacio Zaragoza. Under Zaragoza's command, the Mexican army defeated the French at the Battle of Puebla, a date now celebrated as "Cinco de Mayo" or "Fifth of May" throughout Texas and Mexico. Today the building is filled with exhibits that depict the General's role in Mexican history. Open Friday and Saturday. Free. (512) 645-3752.

Grave of Colonel Fannin and Troops. Just east of the Presidio La Bahia. The large memorial marks the site of the massacre that occurred here on March 27, 1836. Free.

Market House Museum. 202 S. Market. This museum contains exhibits on local history. The building also houses the Goliad Chamber of Commerce, where you can pick up brochures and area maps. Open weekdays. Free. (512) 645-3563.

WHERE TO EAT

La Bahia Restaurant. US 183, south of Presidio La Bahia. Like its name suggests, this restaurant serves Mexican food, from fajitas to tacos, as well as a good selection of steaks and seafood. $-$$; []. (512) 645-3651.

Day Trip 1

ARANSAS PASS
PORT ARANSAS
ROCKPORT-FULTON

Birders come from around the world to test their skill at spotting some of the nearly 500 species recorded in this area.

ARANSAS PASS

To reach Aransas Pass, take I-37 south from San Antonio for 145 miles to Corpus Christi. (For attractions in Corpus Christi, see SOUTH FROM SAN ANTONIO, DAY TRIP 2.) Cross the Harbor Bridge and follow US 181 north to TX 35. Continue to the intersection of TX 361, then turn right to Aransas Pass.

Aransas Pass is more a genuine fishing village and less a tourist destination than many other coastal communities. Most of its 7,000 residents are employed in the fishing industry.

Make your first stop the Chamber of Commerce at 452 Cleveland Boulevard. This office can direct you to the Conn Brown Harbor for a look at the enormous shrimp fleet. The Seamen's Memorial Tower, a monument to the fishermen lost at sea, marks the entrance to the working harbor.

PORT ARANSAS

To reach Port Aransas, follow TX 361 from Aransas Pass across the Redfish Bay causeway to Harbor Island. Look north to see the remains of a lighthouse, abandoned when the channel shifted.

A daily ferry runs 24 hours from Harbor Island across the Corpus Christi Ship Channel to Port Aransas. Port Aransas is located on Mustang Island, named for the wild horses that once roamed here. There's a long wait on weekends during peak season and holidays. Tune your radio to 530 AM for ferry traffic conditions during the morning, lunch hour, and late afternoon rush times.

Port Aransas is a small town filled with year-round seaside attractions. During spring break, "Port A" greets over 150,000 college students from throughout the Midwest and Southwest. The crowds are very manageable the rest of the year, however. During the winter months, most visitors are fishermen and winter Texans.

A fishing cruise is great for a look at the Gulf. Trips include bait and tackle, and cost about $20 a day. Contact the Chamber office for more information.

WHERE TO GO

University of Texas Marine Science Institute. On Ship Channel. Students of oceanography, ecology, marine chemistry, and botany train at this branch of the University of Texas, located on 82 beachfront acres. The Visitors Center is open to the public, featuring exhibits and films on Texas Gulf life. Open weekdays. Free. (512) 749-6720.

Gulf Beach. You can't come to Mustang Island without a trip to the beach. Here swimmers and surfers frequent the shallow warm waters, and souvenir hunters search for fragile sand dollars, pieces of coral, and unbroken shells. Drivers on the public beach are restricted to a marked lane, and parking requires an annual permit, available for $5 from the Chamber of Commerce or at many Port Aransas businesses. There is free boardwalk access to the shoreline from many of the condominiums as well.

Mustang Island State Park. Park Road 53, southwest of Port Aransas. The facilities at this scenic beach include freshwater showers, picnic tables, and tent and RV camping. The area is protected from vehicular traffic. Open daily. Fee. (512) 749-5246.

San Jose Island. Access from Woody's Boat Basin on the Ship Channel. San Jose or "St. Jo" Island is located just north of Mustang Island. It is accessible only by boat and has no restrooms or public facilities. The jetty boats leave from Port Aransas about once an hour from early morning to early evening. Stay all day and enjoy swimming, surfing, or fishing. Open daily. Fee. (512) 749-5252.

Fishing Cruises. Few coastal cities offer more fishing and boating cruises than Port Aransas. In varying seasons, these Gulf waters are home to mackerel, ling, pompano, marlin, barracuda, grouper, and amberjack. In the calmer bay waters, look for redfish, speckled trout, drum, and flounder.

Large fishing boats hold up to 100 passengers, small charters accept a maximum of 6; both depart from the waterfront. Serious fishermen looking for big game fish like marlin and shark should book charter excursions for personalized service. Deposits are required on charters, and credit cards usually are not accepted for the deposit. For information on Port Aransas's many charters, contact the Chamber of Commerce at (800) 45-COAST.

If you take a fishing cruise, be aware that Gulf waters can be very choppy. Except for the bay cruises, most boats travel 15 to 20 miles from shore. Seas are usually calmest in the summer, but even then four- to six-foot waves are possible. Seasickness has spoiled more than one vacationer's cruise, so be sure to purchase motion sickness medication or obtain a skin patch from your doctor before your trip.

Fisherman's Wharf Fishing and Scenic Bay Cruises. Tarpon St. Fisherman's Wharf has two party fishing boats, the *Wharf Cat* and the *Scat Cat*. Both vessels are catamarans, offering a smooth voyage on both half- and full-day deep-water cruises. Tackle and bait are provided, and you won't need a Texas fishing license because fishing is in out-of-state waters. The boats also offer 90-minute cruises of Aransas Bay. Call for a seasonal schedule and for reservations. Fee. (512) 749-5760 or 749-5448.

Island Queen **Cruises.** This converted ferryboat offers bay fishing for speckled trout and redfish. Your ticket includes rod, reel, and tackle. You'll need a Texas fishing license. Call for seasonal schedule. Fee. (512) 749-5252.

Birding Tours. The *Wharf Cat* at Fisherman's Wharf hosts birders from November through March. The cruise leaves Port Aransas for the Aransas National Wildlife Refuge, the winter home of the five-foot-tall whooping cranes. Binoculars and scopes are provided, along with checklists of frequently spotted birds. Reservations are a must. Fee. (512) 749-5760 or 749-5448.

WHERE TO EAT

Tortuga Flats. Trout St., near Fisherman's Wharf. Have a leisurely meal at this dockside restaurant as you watch boats come and go from the harbor. If weather permits, eat outside on the deck. The menu includes oyster "po'boys," shrimp baskets with Texas-sized onion rings, and burgers. Open for lunch and dinner. $$; []. (512) 749-5255.

The Crazy Cajun. 315 Alister St. This Cajun seafood restaurant's house specialty is a steaming concoction of shrimp, sausage, potatoes, stone crab claws, and crawfish in season. The bowl is dumped onto your butcher-paper tablecloth. The atmosphere is casual and fun, and there's live entertainment many nights. Open for lunch and dinner on weekends, dinner only on weekdays; closed Mondays after Labor Day. $$; []. (512) 749-5069.

Seafood and Spaghetti Works. 710 Alister St. This excellent restaurant is housed in a geodesic dome. Spaghetti primavera, shrimp and pepper pasta (a spicy dish that could be called Italian Tex-Mex if there were such a thing), filet mignon, and Cajun-style blackened redfish are popular choices. Save room for the butterfinger cheesecake. Open for dinner only. $$; []. (512) 749-5666.

WHERE TO STAY

You won't find full-service hotels in Port Aransas, but the town does offer everything from luxury condominium complexes to mom-and-pop motels aimed at vacationing fishermen. Many condominiums include full kitchens and appliances, and boardwalk access to the beach.

Sand Castle Condominiums. Sand Castle Dr. This six-story condominium complex is located near the beach. Every room offers a great view and comes with a fully equipped kitchen. (If you can afford it, get a room with a private balcony.) When you've had enough salt water swimming, take a dip in the large free-form pool in the center of the complex. Minimum stay and deposit required. $$$; []. (800) 727-6201.

Tarpon Inn. 200 E. Cotter St. This historic inn is located in a 1923 structure and has breezy porches and large windows. The lobby walls are papered with thousands of tarpon scales, each autographed by the lucky fisherman. There's even a scale signed by Franklin Roosevelt.

The inn's Silver King Restaurant offers chicken-fried steak, steaks, shrimp, and oysters. The restaurant is open for breakfast and lunch from Wednesday through Sunday; dinner also on Thursday, Friday, and Saturday. $$; []. (512) 749-5555 (inn) or 749-4888 (restaurant).

ESPECIALLY FOR WINTER TEXANS

Port Aransas has many activities for winter Texans, from aerobic classes to potluck dinners. Condominiums offer special monthly off-season rates. For a calendar of events or information on rentals, call (800) 452-6278.

ROCKPORT-FULTON

To reach the Rockport-Fulton area, return to Aransas Pass and take TX 35 north for 11 miles.

The adjoining fishing villages of Rockport and Fulton lie along scenic Aransas Bay and are havens for snowbirds of all varieties, from 5-foot-tall whooping cranes to those in 30-foot-long Winnebagos. Both flock to this part of the Texas coast in late October and remain until March. Rockport residents welcome the feathered snowbirds with several protected refuges, and the RVers can take their choice of many well-manicured campgrounds, complete with a friendly small-town atmosphere.

Make your first stop the Rockport-Fulton Area Chamber of Commerce at 404 Broadway. Here you can load up on free brochures and maps, as well as advice from helpful residents.

Rockport and neighboring Fulton have quickly caught the attention of the birding world. In the 1940s, a feisty and dedicated local amateur bird-watcher named Connie Hagar identified hundreds of species. Her research brought Rockport-Fulton to the attention of the National Wildlife Service and other organizations, who eventually recorded nearly 500 species in the area. Today Rockport-Fulton is renowned as one of the finest birding spots in the world.

The Connie Hagar Sanctuary, downtown along TX 35 at Little Bay, is a good place to spot pelicans and many shorebirds. Whooping cranes winter at the Aransas National Wildlife Refuge, northeast of town. The drive to the refuge passes many marshes and coastal plains filled with birds.

Numerous birds fly through the area during fall and winter migration. Every September, Rockport-Fulton hosts a Hummer/Bird Celebration to mark the passage of thousands of hummingbirds who stop through Rockport-Fulton on their way south to Central and South America. Bird lovers from around the country come to watch this feeding frenzy where up to 150 hummingbirds often swarm the same feeder. The annual spring migration each May also brings hundreds of colorful songbirds to the area.

Bird-watching opportunities are available year-round. Contact the Rockport-Fulton Chamber of Commerce to order a copy of the "Birder's Guide." It illustrates the most common species found here, such as pelicans, cranes, storks, and laughing gulls.

Except for year-round boat tours and special bus tours during the Hummer/Bird Celebration, you must depend on self-guided drives to good birding sites. The Chamber can give you directions to the best locations outside of town as well as information about recent spottings.

WHERE TO GO

Texas Maritime Museum. 1202 Navigation Circle, on downtown waterfront. This two-story museum chronicles Texas maritime activities starting with Spanish shipwrecks off the coast and continuing through today's offshore oil industry. Special exhibits are devoted to shipbuilding, Texans of the sea, and the U.S. Army Corps of Engineers. Open Wednesday through Sunday. Fee. (512) 729-1271.

Rockport Art Center. Across the street from Texas Maritime Museum. This restored 1890 house is now the home of the Rockport Art Association and a good place to buy a painting of a Texas beach scene by a local artist. Open Tuesday through Saturday. Free. (512) 729-5519.

Rockport Beach Park. Downtown, just off TX 35. This is a very popular spot, especially during warm weather. The one-mile beach offers swimming, picnicking, boating, fishing, and crabbing off an 800-foot pier, as well as paddleboat and jet ski rentals. There's also a bird-watching platform overlooking a sanctuary area. Open daily. Fee.

Fulton Mansion State Historic Structure. Three miles north of Rockport off TX 35, corner of Henderson St. and Fulton Beach Rd. Built in 1876 by Colonel George Fulton, this grand four-story home overlooks Aransas Bay. It features interesting architecture and surprising modern conveniences.

Built at a cost of $100,000, the house included central forced-air heating. A central cast-iron furnace in the basement provided heat through a series of flues to false, decorative fireplaces in the main rooms. Hot and cold running water was achieved with a tank located in the tower attic. A gas plant located at the back of the house provided fuel for gas chandeliers.

Visitors are asked to wear flat, soft-soled shoes because of delicate Axminster and Brussels carpets purchased from New York. Tours of the home's 29 rooms are conducted Wednesday through Sunday. Fee. (512) 729-0386.

Capt. Ted's *Skimmer*. Adjacent to the Sandollar Pavilion on Fulton Beach Rd. This custom-built tour boat carries birders into shallow waters where many other vessels cannot travel. From November through March, *Skimmer* passengers can view whooping cranes. From April through July, the cruise ventures to nearby islands, including one containing the largest reddish egret rookery in the world. Reservations are required. Fee. Call (800) 338-4551, or write: Star Route 1, P.O. Box 225J, Rockport, TX 78382.

Pisces **Cruises.** Depart from Rockport Harbor. From November through March, this 58-foot vessel conducts whooping crane tours twice daily. The remainder of the year, the *Pisces* operates as a party fishing boat, offering morning and evening four-hour cruises daily in Aransas Bay. Fee. (512) 729-7525.

Goose Island State Recreation Area. TX 35 and Park Road 13, 21 miles northeast of Rockport. The park is home to the state's largest oak tree, the 1,000-year old Lamar Oak. There is camping here, but bring the mosquito repellent during summer months. Fee for camping. (512) 729-2858.

Aransas National Wildlife Refuge. Forty-five minutes northeast of Rockport. Take TX 35 north to FM 774, turn right, and continue to the intersection of FM 2040. Turn right and stay on FM 2040 to the refuge. This 54,829-acre refuge is the prime wintering ground for the endangered whooping crane, plus hundreds of other bird species. The refuge includes several hiking trails and a paved, 15-mile loop drive for a chance to see some of 80 mammal species indigenous to the region: opossum, shrew, bat, armadillo, raccoon, coati, ringtail, mink, weasel, nutria, skink, bobcat, white-tail deer, coyote, and even wild boar.

The observation tower is located on the loop drive. From its heights you can view the elegant whooping cranes, whose numbers once dwindled to only 16. Thanks to conservation programs, the present population has increased tenfold.

The Visitors Center includes films and exhibits on the annual migration of these five-foot-tall birds. Across the road, have a look at native alligators resting in a swampy, fenced enclosure. Open daily. Free. (512) 286-3559.

WHERE TO EAT

The Boiling Pot. Fulton Beach Rd. Don a bib, grab a Mamba beer from one of the 31 Baskin-Robbins-like selections, and sit down. This roadside shack is always noisy and crowded and fun. The Cajun Combo features blue crab, shrimp, andouille sausage, new potatoes, and corn, all boiled up in a spicy pot and dumped from a metal container onto the paper-covered table. You crack the crab claws with a wooden mallet, and dip the succulent flesh in melted butter. Fingers, not forks, are the rule here; dainty eaters need not apply. This is a Texas experience to savor.Open for dinner only from Monday through Thursday; lunch and dinner Friday through Sunday. $-$$; []. (512) 729-6972.

The Sandollar Pavilion. 109 N. Fulton Beach Rd. This restaurant swears the food here is so fresh that "it slept in the ocean last night." Built over the water, the dining room has a beautiful view of Aransas Bay. Call for hours. Open for breakfast, lunch, and dinner, but closed between meals on some days. $$; []. (512) 729-8909.

Austin Street Pub and Eatery. 415 S. Austin St. When you're ready for a break from seafood, head to this casual restaurant for a sizzling plate of fajitas. Open for lunch and dinner daily. $-$$; []. (512) 729-4050.

WHERE TO STAY

Rockport has a huge selection of accommodations, ranging from fishing cottages to elegantly furnished condominiums. Because of the large number of winter Texans who call Rockport home during the cooler months, there are many RV and trailer parks and condominiums that lease by the day, week, or month. For a brochure listing all of Rockport-Fulton's varied lodgings, call the Chamber of Commerce office at (800) 242-0071 or (800) 826-6441 out of state.

Key Allegro Rentals. 1800 Bayshore Dr., just over Key Allegro bridge on Fulton Beach Rd. Key Allegro is a small island linked to Rockport by an arched bridge. The lovely drive to Key Allegro is your first hint at the elegant accommodations awaiting visitors in this area. Nicely appointed condominium units and upscale homes located on the water's edge afford beautiful views of Rockport's fishing vessels heading out for the day's catch. Rental homes and condominiums are available by the day or week. $$-$$$; []. (512) 729-2333 or 729-6588.

Laguna Reef Condos and Hotel. 1021 Water St. This waterfront hotel and condominium resort has an unbeatable view of the bay, especially for early risers who want to watch the gorgeous sunrise. Each fully furnished unit has a private balcony, kitchen, and dining/living room. After a day of sightseeing, take a walk along the complex's beach or down the long fishing pier. The units rent by the day, week, or month. $$; []. (512) 729-1742 or (800) 248-1057.

Kontiki Beach Motel and Condominiums. Fulton Beach Rd. The motel offers spacious accommodations that feature a living and dining area, fully equipped kitchen, and separate bedroom, available by the day, week, or month. Guests also can rent nicely furnished condominiums. All take in a view of the water. Prices vary; []. (800) 242-3407.

ESPECIALLY FOR WINTER TEXANS

Rockport hosts many special events for winter Texans, from fishing to horseshoe tournaments. The town sponsors several winter Texan arts and crafts shows as well as concerts played by talented seasonal residents.

The Paws and Taws Center on Fulton Beach Road is the site of many gatherings for the winter visitors who stay in Rockport and Fulton. With a hardwood floor, a stage, and kitchen facilities, the center holds weekly square dances, bingo games, AARP meetings, and "state days," with parties for visitors from specific states. Chartered bus trips also depart from the center and offer shopping at the border, a tour of German eateries in New Braunfels, outlet shopping in San Marcos, and several other tours.

Fulton sponsors an annual "Welcome Winter Texans" free fish fry in early December.

The Rockport area includes many excellent RV parks, with busy clubhouse activities. For more information, contact the Rockport-Fulton Chamber of Commerce at (800) 242-0071.

Day Trip 2
CORPUS CHRISTI
PADRE AND MUSTANG ISLANDS

CORPUS CHRISTI

To reach Corpus Christi, follow I-37 south for 145 miles from San Antonio. Along the drive, the terrain changes from the rolling hills and shady oaks of the hill country to the grassy flatlands of the coastal plains.

This city of 292,000 residents is a popular year-around destination. During the summer months, the nearby beaches of Padre and Mustang Islands appeal to surfers, families, and sun worshipers. During the winter, this coastal city fills with winter Texans.

The waters of Corpus Christi Bay are calm, protected from the Gulf of Mexico by the barrier islands of Padre and Mustang, which served as pirate hideouts even after the area was chartered in 1519 by Spanish explorer Alonzo Alvarez de Pineda. He bestowed the bay with its name, which means "Body of Christ."

Today Corpus Christi is a thriving city, consistently ranking as America's sixth busiest port. The bayfront is a combination fishing village and tourist spot, and the downtown piers are lined with picturesque shrimp boats. High-rise luxury hotels, specialty shops, and seafood restaurants overlook the bay.

The heart of Corpus Christi is Shoreline Boulevard, with its proud palms and spectacular views of the water. The handsome boulevard begins as Ocean Drive at the gates of the U.S. Naval Air Station and winds north past grand mansions perched on the bluffs overlooking the bay.

Because of the warm weather and a fairly consistent breeze of about 12 miles per hour, Corpus Christi is known as the unofficial windsurfing capital of the United States. Several national regattas are headquartered here, so it's not unusual to see the bay dotted with the colorful sails. Ocean Drive's Oleander Park is the only city-sanctioned sailboard park in the world. If you want to give the sport a try, several operators along South Padre Island Drive offer instruction and rentals.

The north section of Shoreline Boulevard contains the huge piers known as Coopers Street L-Head, Lawrence Street T-Head, and Peoples Street T-Head. Each pier bustles with life, from the predawn hours when the shrimp boats leave until midnight; the night cruises offer fishermen a chance at trophy tarpon, kingfish, or marlin. Peoples Street T-Head is also home of the *Flagship,* an 85-foot paddle wheeler that offers guided bay tours.

The northern end of Shoreline Boulevard also holds the Art Museum of South Texas and the Corpus Christi Museum of Science and History. At the end of the drive is the Harbor Bridge. Built in 1959 to link the city with the small towns that line the Texas coast, it leads across the ship channel to the Texas State Aquarium.

WHERE TO GO

Texas State Aquarium. 2710 Shoreline Dr., across ship channel from downtown area. The Texas State Aquarium focuses on the sea life of the Gulf and the Caribbean Sea, the first such facility in the nation. Phase one of a three-part plan is the Gulf of Mexico Exhibit Building, a $31.5 million facility housing 250 species in over 350,000 gallons of salt water. The 43,000-square-foot building boasts eight major exhibits containing grouper, eels, and sharks. (Two additional phases will add a 300-seat auditorium and a Caribbean Sea Exhibit Building.)

High-tech displays feature the use of a video monitor to help you guide the image of an underwater robotic arm. Touch-screen monitors offer a chance for visitors to try their hand at environmental decision making. When you're finished here, walk outside for a look at the ship channel, the Harbor Bridge, and an unbeatable view of the city. Open daily. Fee. (800) 477-GULF.

Dolphin Connection. Beneath US 181 bridge to Portland, just before Nueces Bay Causeway. Two Dolphin Connection boats take visitors into the bay to feed and interact with dolphins. Owners Erv and Sonja Strong know the wild dolphins by name and are glad to explain their habits, family connections, and life-style. You can hand feed and pet these remarkable mammals during the hour-long excursion. Open daily from March through October or November when the dolphins leave for the winter. Fee. For reservations, call (512) 882-4126, or write: 215 Bridgeport Ave., Suite 4, Corpus Christi, TX 78402.

International Kite Museum. 3200 Surfside Blvd., Best Western Sandy Shores (across Harbor Bridge from downtown). Over 80 exhibits trace the history of the kite and even its use as a military spy tool. Open daily. Free. (512) 883-7456.

Corpus Christi Greyhound Race Track. 5302 Leopard St. Take your chances here with a bet on these fast-as-lightning greyhounds. The atmosphere is very family oriented, although you must be 21 to gamble. The $20 million facility includes a food court and a clubhouse restaurant. The basic entrance fee covers outdoor grandstand seating. During warmer months it's wise to spend a couple of extra bucks for air-conditioned reserved seating, which can be booked six days prior to the race. Open daily. Fee. (800) 580-RACE or (512) 289-9333.

Art Museum of South Texas. 1902 N. Shoreline Blvd., Bayfront Arts and Science Park. Famous for its stark white architecture, this museum is filled with changing fine art exhibits of traditional and contemporary works. Open Tuesday through Sunday. Fee. (512) 884-3844.

Watergardens. Bayfront Arts and Science Park. Here a man-made stream tumbles from the entrance of the art museum down to a sunken circle of flags and fountains. This is a nice place to take a box lunch. Open daily. Free.

Corpus Christi Museum of Science and History. 1900 N. Chaparral, Bayfront Arts and Science Park. This museum is filled with natural history exhibits, including displays recalling the many Spanish shipwrecks found off the Gulf coast. Children can climb aboard a recreation of a 15th-century vessel for a peek at the cramped quarters endured by early explorers. Open Tuesday through Sunday. Fee. (512) 883-2862.

Flagship. Peoples Street T-Head. Several daily tours take visitors for a look at the shipyards and the bay. Sunset cruises are particularly scenic, when the lights of downtown reflect in the calm bay waters. Open daily. Fee. (512) 643-7128 or 884-1693.

Corpus Christi Botanical Gardens. Take S. Staples Dr. south toward Kingsville, past Oso Creek; signs mark entrance. These new gardens feature native South Texas plants and winding trails through the subtropical foliage. Open Tuesday through Sunday. Fee. (512) 852-2100.

WHERE TO EAT

Landry's Dockside. Peoples St. T-Head. This restaurant is a restored two-story barge that sports a casual, fun atmosphere. Murals of fish span the walls, and huge picture windows offer a great view. The specialty of the house is Gulf seafood, including shrimp, oysters, and scallops. Open for lunch and dinner daily. $$; []. (512) 882-6666.

The Lighthouse Restaurant and Oyster Bar. Lawrence St. T-Head. This popular restaurant is shaped like a small lighthouse. From inside, diners have a great view of sailboats on the bay and the Corpus Christi skyline. Seafood and steaks are the specialty here. Open daily for lunch and dinner. $$; []. (512) 883-3982.

Water Street Oyster Bar. 309 N. Water St., Water Street Market. Located just a block from Shoreline Boulevard, this casual restaurant features Cajun-inspired seafood as well as the usual Gulf coast fare. Open daily for lunch and dinner. $$-$$$; []. (512) 881-9448.

WHERE TO STAY

Corpus Christi Marriott Bayfront. 900 N. Shoreline Blvd. This elegant 474-room hotel overlooks the bay and includes a health club, swimming pool, and rooftop dining room. Many of Corpus Christi's main attractions lie within walking distance. $$$; []. (800) 874-4585 or (512) 887-1600.

Embassy Suites Hotel. 4337 S. Padre Island Dr. This all-suite hotel is located on the north side of town, 15 minutes from Shoreline Boulevard and Padre Island. The huge open lobby and atrium include a heated pool, hot tub, and sauna, as well as a dining area that serves a free all-you-can-eat breakfast plus evening cocktails. $$; []. (800) 678-7533 or (512) 853-7899.

ESPECIALLY FOR WINTER TEXANS

If you're in the Corpus Christi area in early February, don't miss the Winterfest, a salute to winter Texans who kick off the festivities by carrying their native flag in the parade of states. Arts and crafts activities, dances, entertainment, and even free medical tests are offered to the many winter Texans who call this stretch of the coast home. For more information, contact the Corpus Christi Convention and Visitors Bureau at (800) 766-BEACH.

PADRE AND MUSTANG ISLANDS

To reach the islands, head out on South Padre Island Drive, also called TX 358. The road is lined with shell shops, windsurfing rentals, bait stands, and car washes. In the shallow waters along the drive, many fishermen stand waist deep in salt water alongside tall herons and pelicans looking for a meal.

When you cross the Intracoastal Waterway via the enormous JFK Causeway Bridge, you leave the mainland for Padre Island. This 110-mile-long barrier island protects much of the Texas coast from hurricanes and tropical storms. Generally, the northern stretch of island paralleling the area from Corpus Christi to Port Mansfield is called Padre Island; from that point to the tip of Texas, the land mass is named *South* Padre Island.

Padre and Mustang Islands feature beaches dotted with rolling dunes, clean sand, and flocks of gulls. The surf is usually gentle and shallow enough to walk for hundreds of yards before reaching chest-deep water. Occasionally undertow is a problem, but on most summer days the waves are gentle and rolling, and the water is warm.

To reach the Padre Island beaches, continue straight on South Padre Island Drive (Park Road 22). Visitors find several parks here from which to choose, each with its own special charm. One of these, the Padre Balli Park, is named for the priest who managed a ranch on the island in the early 19th century. It has a 1,200-foot fishing pier. The Padre Island National Seashore has a snack bar, and showers are available at Malaquite Beach. Although vehicles are allowed on most Padre beaches, Malaquite is one are where vehicles are not permitted.

Beyond Malaquite lies 66 miles of protected beach in Padre Island National Seashore that is accessible only by four-wheel drive vehicles. Little Shell and Big Shell beaches are located in this area, both named because of the wealth of seashells found on their pristine sands.

Although much of Padre Island is undeveloped, you'll find many commercial establishments on neighboring Mustang Island. To reach this barrier island, turn left off South Padre Island Drive from Corpus Christi onto Park Road 53. Only 18 miles long, Mustang Island is far smaller than its neighbor to the south, but it shares many of the same attractions. One of the best stops is Mustang Island State Park, where showers, restrooms, and camping are available. Cars, however, are prohibited on the beach. (For more information on Mustang Island, read SOUTH FROM SAN ANTONIO, DAY TRIP 1.)

Whether you choose Mustang or Padre, follow a few rules of safety. Portuguese man-of-war jellyfish are commonly seen on the beaches. Resist the urge to touch these iridescent purple creatures—their tentacles produce a nasty sting. If you are stung, locals claim the best relief is a paste of meat tenderizer and water applied to the bite.

A far less dangerous, but very annoying, aspect of the Gulf beaches are tar balls. These black clumps, formed by natural seepage and offshore oil spills, wash up on the beach and stick to your skin and your shoes. Many hotels have a tar removal station near the door to help you remove the sticky substance.

WHERE TO GO

Mustang Island State Park. Park Road 53. Mustang Island State Park is clean and enjoyable, perfect for a weekend of RV or tent camping or just a few hours of beachcombing. Freshwater showers are available. Covered picnic tables help keep your gear out of the sand. Open daily. Fee. (512) 749-5246.

WHERE TO STAY

Holiday Inn North Padre Island. 15202 Windward Dr. Here you can walk from the hotel directly to the beach. When you've had enough salt water, have a dip in the hotel swimming pool. $$; []. (800) HOLIDAY or (512) 949-8041.

Island House. 15340 Leeward Dr., Padre Island. This beachfront condominium resort has well-furnished units, many with beautiful views of the Gulf. Each includes a furnished kitchen, a dining/living room, and two bedrooms. Spend the extra money for an oceanfront condo, with sliding glass doors in the living room and the master bedroom, and fall asleep to the sound of waves. $$$; []. (800) 333-8806.

Day Trip 1

LAREDO
NUEVO LAREDO, MEXICO

LAREDO

The 153-mile drive from San Antonio to Laredo via I-35 is a fast one. Although a few small towns appear on this stretch, much of the area remains ranchland.

This city of 120,000 has long been known as the South Texas party spot. It's a popular weekend trip with college students, shoppers, and anyone in search of fun. Built on the banks of the Rio Grande, Laredo dates back to 1755. It was founded by an officer of the Royal Army of Spain, and it was one of the first cities established in this part of the country.

Following the war with Mexico, many Laredo residents packed up and headed across the border to start their own city in Mexico. They named the fledgling community "Nuevo Laredo" or "New Laredo." Healthy trade between the United States and Mexico and the fact that many families boast members on both sides of the border have linked the cities. Thus the nickname: Los Dos Laredos, The Two Laredos.

To reach Laredo's downtown district, take the last exit off I-35 and drive along a narrow, one-way avenue called Zaragoza Street. With its old buildings, constant traffic, and stately palms, the street has a definite Mexican feel. On the right is the enormous St. Augustine Church, founded in 1778. The church overlooks the St. Augustine Plaza, a popular place just to sit and watch the flurry of activity near the bridge.

WHERE TO GO

Museum of the Republic of the Rio Grande. 1009 Zaragoza St., adjacent to the La Posada hotel. Six flags have flown over most of Texas, but Laredo has seen seven, thanks to the brief Republic of the Rio Grande. This museum is housed in one-story adobe structure that was once the capitol building of the Republic of the Rio Grande, a country formed when Northern Mexico seceded from Mexico in 1839. The new state existed until 1841. The museum contains guns, saddles, and household belongings from that brief period. Open Tuesday through Sunday. Free. (210) 727-3480.

Walking Tour of Laredo. The streets of Laredo are lined with historic structures, including many old churches and homes built in the Mexican vernacular and Victorian styles. Self-guided walking tour brochures are available from the Chamber of Commerce. Free. (800) 292-2122.

WHERE TO EAT AND STAY

La Posada. 1000 Zaragoza St. This 224-room hotel is the closest accommodation to the International Bridge leading from Laredo into Mexico. Two Spanish-style courtyards feature tall palms, blooming bougainvillea, and pools, one with a swim-up bar. A relaxed lobby restaurant specializes in Mexican dishes. Restaurant prices vary from $-$$; rooms $$-$$$; []. (800) 292-5659 in Texas; (800) 531-7156 outside the state.

NUEVO LAREDO, MEXICO

Visitors can cross the border into Mexico by car or on foot (the more popular choice). There's no problem driving across at either International Bridge No. 1, also known as the Old Bridge, or International Bridge No. 2, the I-35 bridge.

Nuevo Laredo, with over 300,000 inhabitants, is far larger than its American sister. The city engages in an enormous import-export business, and holds the title as the largest port of entry on the Mexico-U.S. border. A seemingly endless procession of trucks crosses the I-35 bridge all day and night.

Before leaving Laredo, drivers should invest in short-term Mexican auto insurance. Two companies carrying this coverage are Sanborn's U.S.-Mexico Insurance Service at 2212 Santa Ursula (210-722-0931 or 800-442-7286 out of state) and Camper Center Mexican Insurance Agency at 3001 San Bernardo (210-722-0141). Be sure to read the "Entering Mexico" appendix in this book for details on Mexican insurance, proof of citizenship, and prohibited goods.

Most vacationers make the five-minute walk across International Bridge No. 1 to get a better view of the Rio Grande below. In the middle of the bridge is a plaque that marks the border between the two countries.

Cross over the bridge to the shopping district and Avenida Guerrero, where street vendors hawk everything from chewing gum and paper flowers to tablecloths and strands of garlic. In the downtown area, every road parallel to Guerrero is an avenue or *avenida;* one running perpendicular to the avenues (and parallel to the river) is a street or *calle.*

To call Nuevo Laredo telephone numbers, first dial the international code (011), then the country code (52), followed by the phone number.

WHERE TO GO

Turf Club. Calle Bravo and Avenida Ocampo, a few blocks from Nuevo Mercado. This air-conditioned club has live off-track betting, plus a restaurant and bar on the premises. Open daily. (871) 2-0494.

WHERE TO SHOP

Nuevo Mercado. Avenida Guerrero, four blocks from the International Bridge. The *mercado,* or market, is the one place that all tourists visit. Here you find many familiar American faces, English-speaking shopkeepers, and a very friendly atmosphere.

Built around two open courtyards filled with umbrella-shaded tables, the two-story market sells just about every imaginable Mexican-made product. Frozen margaritas and Corona beer are in evidence everywhere, offering a chance to cool down after several hours in the stores. Most shops have no air conditioning, even though summer days often top 100 degrees. Open daily.

Apache Gift Shop. Avenida Matamoros 412, Market Plaza Morales behind Nuevo Mercado. This shop has some unique items not found in the market, including hand-painted clothing, fine silver jewelry, and leather purses. Open daily. (871) 2-6173.

Vega's. Avenida Guerrero, three blocks past the International Bridge. Mexican home furnishings for every room of the house are sold in this well-stocked store. Much of the furniture is hand carved and offered at a price far lower than you'd see in the U.S. Open daily. (871) 4-0775.

Marti's. Avenida Guerrero, three blocks past the International Bridge. This upscale, air-conditioned shop is the nicest store in Nuevo Laredo and the priciest. You don't get a chance to bargain here, so you have to be content with the fact that you're buying the finest jewelry, furnishings, and clothing that Nuevo Laredo has to offer. This place is a favorite with both wealthy Mexicans and South Texas shoppers looking for something above the usual mercado fare. Open daily. (871) 2-3137.

WHERE TO EAT

El Dorado formerly the Cadillac Bar. Calle Belden and Avenida Ocampo, about two blocks from the Mercado. For some travelers, the El Dorado is reason enough to come to Nuevo Laredo. The favorite watering hole for many South Texans, it's the home of the Ramos Gin Fizz, a concoction of gin, lemon juice, and powdered sugar. The menu includes frog legs and red snapper. $$; []. (871) 2-0015.

Victoria 20-30. Calle Victoria, near Nuevo Mercado. This remodeled home-turned-restaurant is now adorned with thick, aqua-tinted windows, a pastel interior, and a forest of plants. Sip a beverage from a hand-blown glass and dine in air-conditioned comfort in one of Nuevo Laredo's most beautiful restaurants, specializing in Tex-Mex favorites such as *cabrito* (barbecued goat). $$; []. (871) 3-3020.

Day Trip 1

EAGLE PASS
PIEDRAS NEGRAS, MEXICO

EAGLE PASS

It's 142 miles southwest on US 57 from San Antonio to Eagle Pass and its sister city, Piedras Negras. These destinations are popular for a weekend of shopping, partying, and south-of-the-border fun.

Eagle Pass, a city of over 25,000 residents, was founded after the Texas Revolution when Mexico prohibited all trade with Texas. Smugglers began a new route to the north. The Texas militia set up an observation camp at a crossing called Paso del Aguila or Eagle Pass, named for eagles nesting in the area. Soon settlers began coming to the area. In 1849 the U.S. Infantry built Fort Duncan to defend the new territory from Indian attack. The fort later was used during the Civil War and manned by Confederate soldiers.

Like other border towns, Eagle Pass is bilingual. Many Mexican citizens cross the border to shop at the large Mall de las Aguilas and in the downtown dress and specialty shops.

For Americans, much of Eagle Pass's appeal lies in its proximity to Mexico. Many visitors spend the cooler hours shopping in Piedras Negras, then return to Eagle Pass for a swim and an evening meal.

WHERE TO GO

Fort Duncan Park. From Main St. (US 57), turn south on South Adams St. Here you can take a self-guided tour of 11 original structures, including barracks and the headquarters building that's home to the Fort Duncan Museum. The museum presents displays on the early history of the old Indian fort and Confederate outpost. The fort saw its final action from 1890 to 1916, when National Guard units were attached to the command following disturbances in Mexico. Open Monday through Friday afternoon or by appointment. Free. (210) 773-2748.

WHERE TO EAT

Kettle Restaurant. 2525 Main St. (US 57) in front of La Quinta Inn. This chain restaurant is open 24 hours a day for breakfast, lunch, and dinner. $$; []. (210) 773-7263.

Charcoal Grill. Mall de las Aguilas, 455 S. Bibb (off US 57). This family-style restaurant specializes in charcoal-grilled steaks and burgers, all brought to your table with a bowl of sliced jalapeños. $$; []. (210) 773-8023.

WHERE TO STAY

La Quinta Motor Inn. 2525 Main St. (US 57). This comfortable family motel, offering a palm-shaded swimming pool, sits just five minutes from the border. $$; []. (800) 531-5900.

PIEDRAS NEGRAS, MEXICO

From Eagle Pass, you can walk or drive across the International Bridge to Piedras Negras, named for the "black rock," or anthracite, found in the area after flooding on the Rio Grande. This city of over 100,000 residents is a gateway to interior Mexico for many tourists, who follow Mexico Highway 57 to Saltillo.

Drivers must purchase short-term Mexican auto insurance before entering Mexico. (American insurance policies are generally not valid in Mexico, where automobile mishaps are a criminal rather than a civil offense.) Coverage is available from Capitol Insurance at 1115 Main Street in Eagle Pass (210-773-2341). (See the appendix "Entering Mexico" in this book for more information.)

Across the border, it's best to use secured parking, available for a small fee on the Plaza Principal, the Main Square, and at several restaurants and motels in town.

In Piedras Negras, as in other border towns, you may drink the water in the better hotels and restaurants. In other establishments, order bottled water or bring your own.

Piedra Negras's Main Square is filled with park benches, stately shade trees, and vendors selling food and drink. It's a nice place to sit for a while and watch the fascinating activity that is Old Mexico.

From the Main Square, follow Zaragoza Street to the Mercado Municipal Zaragoza, the primary tourist market about three blocks away. The walk takes you past Mexican music stores, several bars, *zapatos* (shoe stores) and *ropas* (dress shops). Don't be shocked when you see a tag of $150,000 on a dress; those prices are marked in pesos. (Although the exchange rate fluctuates, one dollar is worth over 3,000 pesos.)

Within the market, goods are marked in both dollars and pesos. The prices are open to *negociación,* a traditional way to purchase items in Mexico. T-shirts, Mexican dresses, serapes, blankets, chess sets, and men's Mexican wedding shirts are all very popular choices in the mercado. (See the "Shopping in Mexico" appendix in this book for pointers.)

To dial a number in Piedras Negras from the United States, first dial the international code (011), then the country code (52), then the telephone number.

WHERE TO STAY

La Quinta Motor Inn. Avenue E. Carranza 1205. This family motel, located a few miles from the market area, includes a restaurant and bar. All 54 rooms are air-conditioned and include cable TV and telephones. $; []. (878) 2-2154.

Casa Blanca. Avenue Lazaro Cardenas (south Mexico Hwy. 57). This white motel is located about 15 minutes from the market area. All rooms are air conditioned and include a television and telephone. The motel also has a beautiful swimming pool and courtyard. $$; []. (878) 2-4646.

Day Trip 2

CASTROVILLE
UVALDE
CONCAN

CASTROVILLE

Castroville is only 20 miles west of San Antonio on US 90, but it's another world in terms of mood and atmosphere. This small town is a mixture of many cultures: French, German, English, Alsatian, and Spanish. It's best known for its Alsatian roots and sometimes is called "The Little Alsace of Texas."

The community was founded by Frenchman Henri Castro, who contracted with the Republic of Texas to bring settlers from Europe. These pioneers came from the French province of Alsace in 1844, bringing with them the Alsatian language, a Germanic dialect. Today only the older residents of Castroville carry on this mother tongue.

Although the language has dropped out of everyday use, many other Alsatian customs and traditions have survived. The city still sports European-style homes with nonsymmetrical, sloping roofs. The Alsatian Dancers of Texas perform folk dancing at many festivals, including San Antonio's Texas Folklife Festival in September. (See "Festivals and Celebrations" at the back of this book.)

Castroville is usually busy on weekends, as San Antonio residents come to shop the town's numerous antique stores, dine in the Alsatian restaurants, and tour the historical sites.

WHERE TO GO

Landmark Inn State Historical Park. 402 Florence St. The Texas Parks and Wildlife Department operates the historic Landmark Inn and museum. The inn was first a home and general store before becoming the Vance Hotel. Robert E. Lee and Bigfoot Wallace, a famous Texas Ranger, were said to have stayed here on the banks of the Medina River.

During World War II the hotel was renamed the Landmark Inn. Aside from accommodations (see "Where to Stay"), the inn contains displays illustrating Henri Castro's early efforts to recruit settlers, as well as exhibits covering early

Castroville life. Also recommended is a self-guided tour of the beautifully manicured inn grounds. Open daily. Free. (210) 538-2133.

Castroville Walking Tour. Pick up a free map from the Chamber of Commerce to see 65 points of interest, from Civil War-era homes to an 1870 brewery. (210) 538-3142.

WHERE TO EAT

Alsatian Restaurant. 403 Angelo St. Housed in a historic 19th-century cottage typical of the provincial homes of Castroville, this restaurant specializes in Alsatian and German food, including spicy Alsatian sausage, crusty French bread, homemade noodles, and red sauerkraut. Steaks and seafood also are served. If it's a nice day, don't miss the chance to dine outside in the open-air biergarten. Open daily for lunch; dinner Thursday through Sunday. $$; []. (210) 538-3260.

WHERE TO STAY

Landmark Inn. 402 Florence St. This historic inn is a terrific place to stay except during the heat of the summer (there's no air conditioning). Guests can stay in one of eight beautifully appointed inn rooms as well as in a separate cottage that once served as the only bath house between San Antonio and Eagle Pass. Most rooms come with private baths; none have telephones. Make your reservations early, especially for weekends. $; no []. (210) 538-2133.

UVALDE

To reach Uvalde, continue west on US 90 through the communities of Hondo, Sabinal, and Knippa. Uvalde is located on the Leona River in the last outreaches of the hill country.

Spanish settlers came to this area in 1674. A century later they attempted to construct missions to convert the Lipan-Apache Indians, the foremost of the Apache groups in Texas. This plan was soon abandoned because of repeated Indian attacks on the mission. The Apaches were defeated in 1709 by Spanish military leader Juan del Uvalde in what's now known as Uvalde Canyon.

WHERE TO GO

Garner Museum. 333 N. Park St. This was once the home of Uvalde's most famous citizen: John Nance Garner, vice president of the United States during Franklin Roosevelt's first and second presidential terms. The museum is filled with reminders of Garner's political career. Open Monday through Saturday. Fee. (210) 278-5018.

CONCAN

WHERE TO GO

Garner State Park. Thirty-one miles north of Uvalde on US 83. Named for John Nance Garner, this beautiful state park is located on the chilly, spring-fed waters of the Frio River (*frio* means cold in Spanish.) There are campsites, screened shelters, cabins with double beds, an 18-hole miniature golf course, and a one-mile hiking trail built by the Civilian Conservation Corps during the 1930s. The highlight of the park is the river, filled with swimmers, inner-tubers, and paddleboats during the warmer months. Open daily. Fee. For reservations, call (210) 232-6132, or write: Garner State Park, HCR #70, P.O. Box 599, Concan, TX 78838.

Day Trip 3

BRACKETTVILLE
DEL RIO
CIUDAD ACUÑA, MEXICO
SEMINOLE CANYON
STATE HISTORICAL PARK

This weekend trip has a lot to offer, from shoot-'em-up fun at Alamo Village to an afternoon dip in Del Rio's San Felipe Springs. Hop across the border for some bargain shopping, a margarita, and a Mexican dinner in Ciudad Acuña. The next day, take your choice of Del Rio's historic sites, a cruise on Lake Amistad, or a look at prehistoric drawings in Seminole Canyon.

BRACKETTVILLE

It's a quick 120 miles down US 90 from San Antonio to Brackettville. (For attractions along this highway, see WEST FROM SAN ANTONIO, DAY TRIP 2.)

Brackettville is the home of Fort Clark, built by the U.S. Cavalry in 1852 to protect the frontier from hostile Indians. Several important soldiers were stationed here over the years, including General George S. Patton. During World War II, Fort Clark served as a German POW camp. At the conclusion of that war, the fort was deactivated.

Fort Clark's military days may be over, but today the compound has taken on a new role as a resort, its stone barracks converted to modern motel rooms. There's also an RV park nearby.

WHERE TO GO

Old Guardhouse Jail Cavalry Museum. US 90, in Fort Clark Springs. Famous generals who served at Fort Clark are featured in this museum, along with the many troops who passed through the post. Open weekend afternoons. Free. (210) 563-2493.

Alamo Village. North of Brackettville; turn off US 90 on FM 674 and continue for seven miles. This family amusement theme park, located on a 30-square-mile ranch, is often used as a movie set. It features a replica of the Alamo, built in the mid-1950s for the filming of *The Alamo,* starring John Wayne. Since that time, many movies, commercials, documentaries, and TV shows have been shot here.

While there are no amusement rides, visitors can tour the John Wayne Museum, filled with pictures and posters from his many films, as well as an Old West jail (complete with cells), a blacksmith's shop, a chapel, and a bank that's been the scene of many movie holdups. During summer months, gunslingers bite the dust four times a day at showdowns staged in front of the cantina. Open daily except the Christmas holidays. Fee. (210) 563-2580.

WHERE TO STAY

Fort Clark Springs Motel and RV Park. US 90, in Fort Clark Springs. The stone barracks of this 1872 fort have been renovated into modern motel rooms. Guests have access to a pool, plus 9- and 18-hole golf courses. $$; []. (210) 563-2493.

DEL RIO

Located 32 miles west on US 90 from Brackettville, Del Rio is the most popular border town within reach of San Antonio. It's a year-round paradise for fishermen, hunters, boaters, and archaeology buffs. Many Texas border towns serve primarily as overnight stops after a day in Mexico, but Del Rio is its own main attraction. Museums, historic sites, fishing, camping, bird-watching, and boating are all within 30 minutes of downtown.

Another feature that separates Del Rio from other border cities is its abundance of water. The town is literally an oasis in the semiarid climate at the edge of the Chihuahuan Desert. Tall palm trees, lush lawns, and golf courses dotted with water hazards are seen throughout the city. The San Felipe Springs pump 90 million gallons of water daily. The crystal-clear water has drawn inhabitants to this region for 10,000 years, from prehistoric Indians who lived in the canyons west of here to Spanish missionaries who named the area "San Felipe del Rio" in 1635.

Today the San Felipe Springs provide water for the city of Del Rio, offering a cool swim on a hot summer day. At the new San Felipe Amphitheater, the water is diverted through a stone moat separating the audience from a stage used for concerts and special events.

Del Rio lies 12 miles from the Amistad Dam and Lake Amistad, both the result of a cooperative effort between Mexico and the United States.

WHERE TO GO

Val Verde Winery. 100 Qualia Dr. Italian immigrant Frank Qualia established this winery in 1883, drawn to the area by its flowing springs and fertile land. The oldest winery in Texas, this enterprise is now operated by third generation vintner Thomas Qualia. Val Verde produces seven wines, including award-winning Don Luis Tawny Port. Tours and tastings are available on a drop-in basis. Open daily except Sundays. Free. (210) 775-9714.

Whitehead Memorial Museum. 1308 S. Main St. This museum is best known for its replica of the Jersey Lilly, Judge Roy Bean's saloon and courtroom. (The original Jersey Lilly remains in Langtry, about 60 miles west of Del Rio.) Judge Bean and his son Sam are buried behind the replica of the saloon, their graves marked with simple headstones. Open Tuesday through Saturday. Fee. (210) 774-7568.

Lake Amistad. West of Del Rio on US 90. The construction of Lake Amistad (derived from the Spanish word for "friendship") was a cooperative project between the United States and Mexico. The 67,000-acre lake was completed in 1969 as a way to control flooding, provide irrigation for South Texas farms and ranches, and offer water recreation. Surrounded by 1,000 miles of shoreline, the reservoir contains striper, bass, crappie, perch, catfish, gar, and sunfish. You must have separate fishing licenses for the U.S. and Mexican areas of the lake. Both Texas and Mexico fishing licenses are sold in the marinas and in many Del Rio stores.

The six-mile-long Amistad Dam is responsible for the creation of the enormous lake. The observation deck affords a look at the 86-mile-long reservoir. Atop the dam stand two bronze eagles, each seven feet tall, symbolizing the two participating countries and marking the international border.

Tlaloc, the Rain God. Mexican shore of Lake Amistad, near Amistad Dam. This 23-foot stone statue is a replica of one carved by the Teotihuacán people, years before Aztec rule in Mexico. Tlaloc is believed to bring rain. Some swear the statue works, pointing to the higher than normal rainfalls in the years following the dam's construction.

Lake Amistad Resort and Marina. US 90, Diablo East Recreation Area. Concessioners at the marina rent small powerboats and houseboats sleeping from 6 to 10 people. You can cruise to the main part of Lake Amistad or up the Devil's River to some clear, spring-fed swimming holes. Open daily. Fee. (210) 774-4157.

High Bridge Adventures. Pecos River Boat Ramp, 10 miles west of Comstock. If you want someone else to man the wheel, take a cruise aboard this pontoon boat up the Pecos River and Rio Grande. The tour docks at both Parida and Panther Caves. It's a short walk to see the ancient pictographs drawn by the area's prehistoric residents. The tour takes about 3½ hours, and reservations are required. Open daily year-round. Fee. For reservations, call (915) 292-4495, or write: P.O. Box 816, Comstock, TX 78837.

WHERE TO EAT

Wright's Steak House. US 90, three miles west of the intersection of US 277. This casual steak house features all the usual cuts plus choices like Texas-sized chicken-fried steak. Save room for home-baked cheesecake, then work off that big dinner on the dance floor. Live entertainment appears every Friday and Saturday night. Closed Monday. Dinner only Tuesday through Saturday; lunch and dinner Sunday. $$; []. (210) 775-2621.

The Mexican Kitchen. 807 E. Losoya. This Mexican restaurant is called "The Home of Chimichangas and Flautas," but the cooks also make terrific enchiladas. There's nothing fancy here, just lots of good Tex-Mex food. $; []. (210) 774-2280.

WHERE TO STAY

Del Rio offers a wide array of accommodations, from mom-and-pop motels to popular chains to fishing resorts. For a complete listing, call the Del Rio Chamber of Commerce (210-775-3551), or write: 1915 Ave. F, Del Rio, TX 78840.

Ramada Inn. 2101 Ave. F. This popular 96-room motel is conveniently located on the main thoroughfare through town, offering guests a pool, hot tub, workout room, restaurant, and bar. $$; []. (800) 272-6232 or (210) 775-1511.

ESPECIALLY FOR WINTER TEXANS

Del Rio has a very active winter visitors community. The Chamber of Commerce hosts a Winter Texan Welcome Party, an arts and crafts fair, and an appreciation party during the season.

The Welcome Party is held on the first weekend in December and includes a traditional Texas meal of chili and beans. Exhibits introduce newcomers to local attractions, and gold cards offering discounts at area businesses are distributed.

The Winter Visitors Crafts Fair kicks off in February, giving participants a chance to sell arts and crafts without the usual booth expense associated with such shows. In mid-March, Del Rio hosts a big Winter Visitors Appreciation Party.

The Chamber also publishes a calendar of special events planned for winter visitors, including dessert cook-offs, Mexican shopping trips, museum tours, and more. For a copy, call the Del Rio Chamber at (210) 775-3551.

CIUDAD ACUÑA, MEXICO

To reach the international border and Ciudad Acuña, follow Garfield Avenue (Spur 239) west for three miles. Most travelers drive to the Texas side of the International Bridge and pay a small fee for secured parking. From there, you can take a cab across the river or walk across the toll bridge.

Trolleys also depart from the downtown terminal in Del Rio and take visitors to the U.S. side of the bridge. From there it's a five-minute walk across the border to the retail district in Acuña. The trolleys run every half hour until 6:30 p.m. There's also a bus that carries shoppers from Del Rio across the border to

Acuña's shopping district. For a round-trip trolley and bus schedule, call (512) 774-0580.

Acuña (pronounced "a-COON-ya") is filled with tourist shops, especially along Hidalgo Street. There is no central market here, but the shops are continuous for several blocks as you enter town.

To place telephone calls to Mexico, first dial the international code (011), then the country code (52), followed by the phone number.

WHERE TO SHOP

El Caballo Blanco. Hidalgo 110. This leather shop is filled, floor to ceiling, with handbags, billfolds, huaraches, boots, saddles, and even gun holsters. Look for traditional Mexican purses, hand tooled with cactus, Aztec, and eagle designs. Open daily.

Nick's Warehouse. Hidalgo 185. Nick's calls itself the largest handmade dress shop in Acuña, and it is. Beautifully embroidered items in festive colors fill the racks, from infant clothes to one-size-fits-all women's dresses. Open daily. (877) 2-1631.

Casa Uxmal (Artesanías Mexicanas). Hidalgo 125. This shop has a little of everything, from abalone inlay jewelry and Mexican dresses to hand-blown glass. Open daily. (877) 2-0925.

WHERE TO EAT

Crosbys. Hidalgo 195. Both Americans and Mexicans frequent this lively restaurant for a good meal and a good time. From the etched glass and oak doors to the white columns separating the dining rooms, the look says "elegant" but the atmosphere definitely shouts "party." The menu features Tex-Mex food, steaks, seafood, and *de la presa la Amistad*—fish from nearby Lake Amistad. Try the *Camarón Relleno Estilo Crosbys* (shrimp stuffed with cheese and wrapped in bacon) or share a sampler platter, a massive tray of breaded quail, frog legs, stuffed shrimp, and beef strips. The margaritas are king-sized and served in glasses resembling goldfish bowls.

Service on Friday and Saturday nights can be slow by American standards. Open daily for lunch and dinner. $$; []. (877) 2-2020.

SEMINOLE CANYON STATE HISTORICAL PARK

To reach the entrance of Seminole Canyon State Historical Park, drive west on US 90 from Del Rio, nine miles past the town of Comstock. This is a stop archaeology buffs shouldn't miss. During the warmer months, make this an early morning trip because the canyon can be very hot during the afternoon hours.

Seminole Canyon was occupied by prehistoric man about 8,500 years ago. Little is known of that early culture, but archaeologists believe these people were hunter-gatherers, living on plants and small animals. The former residents left paintings on the caves and canyon walls that represent animals, Indians, and supernatural shamans, but their meaning is still unknown. Sadly, these artifacts are fading, and it is unknown how much longer the images will last. Scientists currently are studying ways to slow the deterioration.

Visitors can see the pictographs on a 90-minute guided tour conducted Wednesday through Sunday at 10 a.m. and 3 p.m. This is a somewhat strenuous one-mile hike, so bring along a small canteen of water (there are no drinking facilities in the canyon). The trip also takes in Fate Bell Shelter, named for the archaeologist who discovered the pictographs.

In the park campground, both tent and trailer sites are available, along with electrical and water hookups. Open daily. Fee. For more information on camping, call (915) 292-4464, or write: Park Superintendent, Seminole Canyon State Historical Park, P.O. Box 820, Comstock, TX 78837.

Day Trip 1

BANDERA
MEDINA
VANDERPOOL

BANDERA

Follow TX 16 northwest for 50 miles to Bandera, "The Cowboy Capital of the World." This town is well known for its plentiful dude ranches, country-western music, rodeos, and horse racing.

Once part of the "Wild West," Bandera Pass, located 12 miles north of town on TX 173, was the site of many battles between Spanish conquistadors and both Apache and Comanche Indians. Legend has it that following a battle with the Apaches in 1732, a flag (or *bandera* in Spanish) was hung at the pass to mark the boundary between the two opposing forces.

Today the wildest action in town occurs in the dance halls on Friday and Saturday nights. Put on your boots, crease your best jeans, and get ready to two-step with locals and vacationers alike.

WHERE TO GO

Frontier Times Museum. 13th St., one block north of courthouse. Established in 1927, this museum is a good place to learn more about Bandera's early days. The stone building is filled with cowboy paraphernalia, Indian arrowheads, and prehistoric artifacts. Its most unusual exhibit is a shrunken head from Ecuador, part of a private collection donated to the museum. Open daily. Fee. (210) 796-3864.

Bandera Downs. TX 16, south of Bandera. Place your bet on your favorite horse at this thoroughbred and quarterhorse track. There's full food service and private seating in the Jockey Club, sports-book seating at the Turf Club Terrace, and open-air seating in the grandstand. Open Friday, Saturday, and Sunday during racing season, March through October. Fee. (210) 796-7781.

Hill Country State Natural Area. South on TX 173 to FM 1077, right for 12 miles. FM 1077 does not appear on the state map, but it is labeled on the free county map available from the Bandera Chamber of Commerce (800-364-3833).

This rugged park preserves 5,000 acres of hill country land. Only primitive camping is available; you must bring your own water, and pick up and remove your own trash. There's also horseback riding, bicycling, and fishing. Open daily except during December and January, when park closes Tuesday and Wednesday. Fee. (210) 796-4413.

Medina River. TX 16, east of town. The cypress-lined Medina River is a popular spot during the summer months, when swimmers, canoeists, and inner-tubers enjoy the cool water. The Medina can be hazardous during high water, however, with rocky rapids and submerged trees. There is public access to the river from the TX 16 bridge in town. For rental or shuttle information or advice on the rapids, call (210) 796-3553.

WHERE TO SHOP

Bandera Forge. 803 Main St. This shop includes a large stock of forged works, including windchimes and boot scrapers. The blacksmith will create a personalized branding iron for you to take back home as a souvenir. Open daily. (210) 796-7184.

WHERE TO STAY

The country around Bandera is dotted with dude ranches. Rates usually include three meals daily, as well as family-style entertainment and supervised children's programs. Horseback riding is often part of the week-long package. A minimum stay of two or three days is required at most ranches during peak summer season.

For a complete listing of Bandera's dude ranches, as well as other accommodations and campgrounds, call the Bandera Chamber of Commerce at (800) 364-3833.

Mayan Ranch. TX 16, two miles west of Bandera. For over 40 years, this 60-room ranch has entertained vacationers with cowboy breakfasts, cookouts, horseback riding, fishing, and hayrides. Summer also brings organized children's programs. Rooms are appointed with Western-style furniture. Call for rates; []. (210) 796-3312 or 796-3036.

Dixie Dude Ranch. South on TX 173 1½ miles to FM 1077, then southwest for nine more miles. Five generations of the Whitley family have welcomed guests to this 19-room ranch since 1937. Rates include meals and two horseback rides daily. Call for rates; []. (210) 796-4481.

Flying L Guest Ranch. From TX 16, turn south on TX 173 for 1½ miles, then left on Wharton Dock Rd. This 542-acre ranch has 38 guest houses, each with two rooms, refrigerator, microwave, coffee pot, and TV. You can choose many different packages offering horseback riding, hayrides, and even golf at the ranch's 18-hole course. During the summer, there's a supervised children's program, plus nightly entertainment that ranges from Western shows to "branding" parties. Call for rates; []. (800) 292-5134.

ESPECIALLY FOR WINTER TEXANS

Besides the dude ranches, Bandera has excellent RV parks. Many weekly activities are of special interest to the winter Texans who call Bandera home. Country-western dances are held Wednesday through Saturday, square dances swing on Mondays, and there's bingo on Fridays. For a complete listing, contact the Bandera Chamber of Commerce at (800) 364-3833.

MEDINA

From Bandera, continue west on TX 16 to the tiny community of Medina, best known for its dwarf apple trees that produce full-sized fruit in varieties from Crispin to Jonagold.

WHERE TO GO

Love Creek Orchards. RR 337, west of Medina. From May through October, these beautiful dwarf apple orchards are open to the public by guided tour only on Saturday mornings. Tours depart at 10 a.m. from the Cider Mill and Country Store on TX 16. Free. (210) 589-2588.

WHERE TO SHOP

The Cider Mill and Country Store. Main St. (TX 16), downtown. This shop offers Love Creek apples for sale from June through November. Butter, sauces, vinegars, jellies, syrups, pies, breads, and even apple ice cream are sold here year-round. If you're ready to start your own orchard but you're short on room, you can buy "the patio apple orchard," a dwarf tree grown on a trellis in a wooden planter. Open daily. (210) 589-2588.

VANDERPOOL

WHERE TO GO

Lost Maples State Natural Area. West on RR 337 to the intersection of RR 187; turn north and continue for five miles. This state park is very popular during the fall when the bigtooth maples provide some of the best color in Texas. Weekend visits during this time can be very crowded.

There are 10 miles of hiking trails to enjoy all year along the Sabinal River Canyon. In the summer visitors can swim and fish in the river. Camping includes primitive areas on the hiking trails and a 30-site campground with restrooms and showers as well as a trailer dump station. Open daily. Fee. (210) 966-3413.

Day Trip 2

KERRVILLE
INGRAM
HUNT
Y. O. RANCH

KERRVILLE

To reach Kerrville from Vanderpool (NORTHWEST FROM SAN ANTONIO, DAY TRIP 1), retrace your steps east to Medina on FM 337 and head north on TX 16. You can also leave San Antonio on I-10, traveling through Boerne and Comfort before exiting at TX 27 for the final 19 miles. If you take this route, be sure to read NORTHWEST FROM SAN ANTONIO, DAY TRIP 3 for attractions in these hill country towns.

Kerrville is popular with retirees, hunters, winter Texans, and campers. The town of 19,000 residents is home to a 500-acre state park and many privately owned camps catering to youth and church groups.

Started in the 1840s, the town was named for James Kerr, a supporter of Texas independence who died in the Civil War. With its unpolluted environment and low humidity, Kerrville later became known as a health center, attracting tuberculosis patients from around the country. The town is still considered one of the most healthful places to live in the nation because of its clean air and moderate climate.

Throughout Kerrville the Schreiner name appears on everything from Schreiner College to Schreiner's Department Store. Charles Schreiner, who became a Texas Ranger at the tender age of 15, came to Kerrville as a young man in the 1850s. Following the Civil War, he began a dry goods store and started acquiring land and raising sheep and goats.

The Charles Schreiner Company soon expanded to include banking, ranching, and marketing wool and mohair. This was the first business in America to recognize the value of mohair, the product of Angora goats. Before long, Schreiner made Kerrville the mohair capital of the world.

In 1880 Schreiner acquired the Y. O. Ranch, which grew over the next 20 years to over 600,000 acres, covering a distance of 80 miles. Today the Schreiner family still owns this well-known ranch, located in nearby Mountain Home.

WHERE TO GO

Cowboy Artists of America Museum. 1550 Bandera Hwy. (TX 173). This hilltop museum features work by members of the Cowboy Artists of America. The building is constructed of 18 *boveda* brick domes, an old construction method used in Mexico. Western-themed paintings and sculpture fill the museum. Visitors also can take in special programs on the folklore, music, and history of the Old West. Open Tuesday through Sunday. Fee. (210) 896-2553.

The Hill Country Museum. 226 Earl Garrett St. This local history museum traces the development of Kerrville. Housed in Charles Schreiner's former mansion built in 1879, the building has granite porch columns, wooden parquet floors, and a bronze fountain imported from France. Open Monday through Saturday. Fee. (210) 896-8633.

Classic Showcase. I-10 at Harper Rd. Here wax figures of World War II heroes Eisenhower, MacArthur, and Patton confer beside a jeep; Jean Harlow steps out of a Brewster; and Henry Ford and George Washington Carver discuss Carver's contributions to the automotive industry. This museum showcases historic automobiles and their use by various celebrities. Closed Tuesday. Fee. (210) 895-5655.

Kerrville State Park. One mile southwest on TX 16. This park offers seven miles of hiking trails, as well as fishing and swimming in the Guadalupe River. Campsites include water, electricity, sewage hookups, and screened shelters. Fee. For reservations, call (210) 257-5392, or write: 2385 Bandera Hwy., Kerrville, TX 78028.

Louise Hays City Park. Off TX 16 at Thompson Dr. Bring your picnic lunch to this beautiful spot on the Guadalupe River. Paddleboats are available for rent, and ducks and cypress trees abound. Days only.

WHERE TO SHOP

Pampell's. 701 Water St. In its 1895 heyday, Pampell Opera House was a lavish venue for musical productions. Today the building is home to an antique store and an old-fashioned soda fountain. Many original furnishings remain, along with items from quilts to elaborate doll house miniatures. At the fountain, take a seat on one of the revolving stools and order up a thick malt or a dish of Brenham's Blue Bell ice cream. Open Monday through Saturday. (210) 257-8484.

James Avery, Craftsman. Off FM 783, north of I-10. Since 1954 James Avery has been one of Texas's premier silversmiths. He began crafting silver crosses and religious symbols, but today his work includes gold and silver renditions of many subjects, from prickly pears to dolphins. Open Monday through Saturday. (210) 895-1122 or 895-6800.

WHERE TO STAY

Y. O. Ranch Hilton. 2033 Sidney Baker, at TX 16 and I-10. This 200-room hotel salutes the famous Y. O. Ranch in Mountain Home, located 30 miles from Kerrville. The lobby is filled with reminders of the area's major industries, cattle and hunting. Twelve hotel suites include amenities such as fireplaces, furniture covered in longhorn hide, and wet bars. In keeping with the Wild West spirit, the hotel has a bar called the Elm Water Hole Saloon and a swim-up bar dubbed the Jersey Lilly. $$; []. (800) 531-2800.

ESPECIALLY FOR WINTER TEXANS

Kerrville is home to over a dozen RV parks, some of which are designated adults only. For a listing, contact the Kerrville Chamber of Commerce at (800) 221-7958 in Texas or (210) 896-1155. This office also can provide a listing of condominium and apartment properties with short-term leases. A welcoming committee greets winter Texans as well as the many retirees who relocate in the area.

INGRAM

To reach Ingram, leave Kerrville on TX 27 and continue northwest for seven miles. This small community on the banks of the Guadalupe River was started in 1879 by Reverend J. C. W. Ingram, who built a general store and post office in what is now called Old Ingram.

Old Ingram, located off TX 27 on Old Ingram Loop, is home to many art galleries and antique shops. Ingram proper lies along TX 27, and it features stores and outfitters catering to white-tail deer, turkey, and quail hunters. The town is particularly busy during deer season, from November to early January.

Hunting licenses are required and are sold at local sporting good stores. For more information, call the Texas Parks and Wildlife Department at (800) 792-1112 in Texas or (210) 389-4800 elsewhere, or write: 4200 Smith School Rd., Austin, TX 78744.

WHERE TO GO

Kerr County Historical Murals. At TX 27 and TX 39. Sixteen murals decorate the T. J. Moore Lumber Company building, the work of local artist Jack Feagan. The scenes portray historical events in Kerr County, starting with the establishment of shingle camps (where wooden roofing shingles were produced in 1846). Other paintings highlight cattle drives, the birth of the mohair industry, and the last Indian raid.

Hill Country Arts Foundation. TX 39, west of the Ingram Loop. Plays, art competitions and exhibitions, art shows, classes, and workshops are offered at this 15-acre facility. A gallery exhibits the work of many artists and is open daily. The Gazebo Gift Shop is a sales outlet for local artists, open Monday through Friday afternoons. Call for a schedule of play times or special events. (210) 367-5121.

WHERE TO SHOP

Guadalupe Forge. TX 27, just off TX 39. You can have your own brand made in this blacksmith shop, the walls of which are decorated with cattle brands ranging from simple initials to more elaborate renderings of stars or the rising sun. Open Monday through Saturday. (210) 367-4433.

Southwestern Elegance. Old Ingram Loop. This unique store specializes in Mexican collectibles and antiques (especially primitives), Mennonite furniture, and Tarahumara Indian collectibles. Open daily; call for hours. (210) 367-4749.

HUNT

Continue west on TX 39 for seven miles to Hunt, a small community best known for its year-round outdoor recreational camps catering to Scouts as well as youth and church groups.

WHERE TO GO

Crider's Rodeo and Dance Hall. TX 39, three miles southwest of Hunt. Here's your chance to kick up your heels Texas-style on a wooden dance floor. This popular establishment opened in 1925 and continued on through Prohibition, when moonshine was sold in the parking lot. Today the dance hall, and nearby rodeo, are open May through September. Fee. (210) 238-4874.

Stonehenge II. FM 1340, just out of Hunt. Located on private land, this replica of England's Stonehenge may be viewed from a roadside parking area. A sign provides information on the original Stonehenge and its smaller Texas cousin. Open daily. Free.

Y. O. RANCH

From Hunt, head west on FM 1340 to TX 41. Turn left and the Y. O. Ranch will soon appear on your right. This ranch dates back to 1880, a part of the 550,000 acres purchased by Captain Charles Schreiner, former Texas Ranger and longhorn cattle owner.

Presently the Y. O. spans 60 square miles and supports over 1,000 registered longhorns, the largest such herd in the nation. Charlie Schreiner III, the original owner's grandson, brought the breed back from near extinction in the late 1950s, founding the Texas Longhorn Breeders Association. The Y. O. hosts a longhorn trail drive at the ranch each spring.

After the devastating Texas drought in the 1950s, the Schreiners began to diversify the use of their ranch, stocking the land with the largest collection of natural roaming exotics in the country, including many rare and endangered species. Over 10,000 animals range the hills, including zebra, ostrich, giraffe, emu, and ibex.

You may visit the Y. O. Ranch by reservation only. Both day and overnight programs are offered. Day trippers can enjoy the ranch on a lunch tour or photo safari. The ranch also hosts an Outdoor Awareness Program, an environmental education camp teaching horseback riding, rappelling, gun handling, and wildlife study. For general information, call (210) 640-3348; for information on a day visit or overnight stay, call (210) 640-3222.

Day Trip 3

BOERNE
COMFORT
SISTERDALE

This is an easy day trip from San Antonio, a journey through three small towns that share a strong German heritage. Although the excursion begins on sleek I-10, it includes some curving farm-to-market roads that are very susceptible to flooding. If it's raining heavily, save this trip for another day!

BOERNE

To reach Boerne (pronounced "BURR-nee"), take I-10 northwest for 22 miles to a small town filled with history, antiques, and natural attractions.

Boerne is located on the banks of Cibolo Creek in the rolling Texas hill country. The community was founded in 1847 by German immigrants, members of the same group who settled nearby New Braunfels. They named the town for author Ludwig Boerne, whose writings inspired many men to leave Germany for the New World.

During the 1880s, Boerne became known as a health spot, and vacationers came by railroad to soak in mineral water spas and enjoy the clean country air. Although no mineral spas remain today, Boerne still offers a quiet country atmosphere and dozens of antique shops in which to browse.

WHERE TO GO

Chamber of Commerce. One Main Plaza, beside Ye Kendall Inn. Stop here for brochures and maps to Boerne attractions and shopping areas. Open daily Monday through Friday, and Saturday morning. (210) 249-8000.

Agricultural Heritage Center. TX 46, one mile from Main St. This museum features farm and ranch tools used by pioneers in the late 19th and early 20th centuries, including a working steam-operated blacksmith shop. Six acres surrounding the museum are covered with hand-drawn plows, wagons, early tractors, and woodworking tools. Open Sunday and Wednesday afternoons. Free. (210) 249-8000.

Cascade Caverns. From I-10 take exit 543 and follow signs on Cascade Caverns Rd. This family-owned cavern has a 100-foot waterfall, an unusual underground sight. Guided tours take 45 minutes. For those who wish to stay longer, there's an RV park on site as well. Open daily. Fee. (210) 755-8080.

Cave Without A Name. TX 474 north for eight miles to Kreutzberg Rd., follow signs for five miles. This 50-million-year-old cave is privately owned and, while not as well known as other hill country caverns, boasts many beautiful formations. A 45-minute tour takes you through a series of rooms, including one with Texas-sized stalagmites. Graveled walks wind through the cavern, and no difficult climbing is necessary. Tours are given as often as visitors arrive. Call ahead. Closed Tuesdays. Fee. (210) 537-4212.

WHERE TO EAT

Ye Kendall Inn. 128 W. Blanco St., Main Plaza. In 1859 the owners of this two-story structure began renting rooms to stagecoach travelers, eventually developing the property into an inn. Over the years, its famous guests have included Confederate President Jefferson Davis and President Dwight D. Eisenhower. Along with seven bed and breakfast rooms furnished with period antiques, the inn includes a restaurant with adjoining bar that serves favorites such as burgers, salads, and soups along with specialties like lemon chicken schnitzel, chicken-fried steak, and Gulf shrimp. Open daily for lunch and dinner. $$; []. (210) 249-2138.

ESPECIALLY FOR WINTER TEXANS

Cascade Caverns Campgrounds. Campers visiting this beautiful 105-acre park surrounding Cascade Caverns find RV sites with hookups, barbecue pits, and picnic tables. Shower facilities, a dance hall, volleyball and badminton courts, and pool tables also are available. Fee. (210) 755-8080.

COMFORT

From Boerne, continue north on I-10 for 17 miles to the town of Comfort. This small community is big in history and attractions. The downtown area is a National Historic District, filled with homes and businesses built by early settlers.

Comfort was founded by German pioneers in 1854 who wanted to name the town "Gemuetlichkeit," meaning peace, serenity, comfort, and happiness. After some deliberation, though, they decided on the easier-to-pronounce "Comfort" instead.

Today Comfort offers tourists numerous historic buildings to explore, filled with antique shops and restaurants. Visitors also find a historic inn and the oldest general store in Texas. Weekends are the busiest time to visit, but even then the atmosphere is relaxing, unhurried, and, well, comfortable.

WHERE TO GO

"Treue der Union" (True to the Union) Monument. High St., between Third and Fourth Sts. During the Civil War, German residents of Comfort who did not approve of slavery and openly swore their loyalty to the Union were burned out of their farms. The Confederates responsible also lynched locals who refused to pledge their allegiance to the movement. Several German farmers decided to defect to Mexico but were caught by Confederate soldiers and killed on the banks of the Nueces River, their bodies left unburied.

Finally retrieved in 1865, their remains were returned to Comfort and buried in a mass grave. A white obelisk, the oldest monument in Texas and the only monument to the Union located south of the Mason-Dixon line, was dedicated here in 1866. One of only six such sites in the country, the shrine recently received Congressional approval to continually fly the flag at half mast. The flag that waves here has 36 stars, the same number it had when the marker was dedicated in 1866. Free.

Ingenhuett Store. 830 High St. Built in 1880 by Peter Ingenhuett, this general store is now operated by fourth and fifth generation family members. One of the oldest continually operated general stores in Texas, this place is busy all the time! Don't miss the Ingenhuett history display, complete with photos of the Ingenhuett ancestors and Comfort's early days. Closed Sunday. Free. (210) 995-2149.

Bat Roost. FM 473, on private land. As you leave Comfort for Sisterdale, this historic structure sits one mile from town on the right side of the road behind private gates. While it's generally known now that bats feed on disease-spreading mosquitoes, the folks here have known about the importance of these furry mammals since 1918, when Albert Steves constructed hygieostatic bat roosts in an experimental attempt to control malaria. The roosts were intended to encourage the area's large bat population to remain in the region. Only 16 such roosts were built in the country, and this is the oldest of three known still to exist. Free (at present visitors are not allowed to enter property).

WHERE TO SHOP

The Comfort Common. 818 High St. This combination bed and breakfast inn and indoor shopping area is located within the historic Ingenhuett-Faust Hotel. Several buildings behind the hotel display antique primitives and furniture. Open daily. (210) 995-3030.

Bygone Days. 408 Seventh St. This year-round Christmas store features handmade Santa Claus figures as well as numerous antiques, all in a historic building with original counters and fixtures. Open Tuesday through Saturday. (210) 995-3003.

Martketplatz. Seventh and Main Sts. This large antique store offers two floors of furniture, collectibles, quilts, and crafts. Open Tuesday through Saturday, and Sunday afternoon. (210) 995-2000.

WHERE TO STAY

The Comfort Common. 818 High St. This bed and breakfast operates within the 1880 Ingenhuett-Faust Hotel. The five suites are decorated in English country, American country, and Victorian decor. All rooms include private baths and period furnishings. The backyard cottage has a fireplace and complete kitchen. All rates include breakfast. As rooms book quickly for weekends, consider a mid-week stay. $$; []. (210) 995-3030.

SISTERDALE

WHERE TO GO

Sister Creek Vineyards. FM 1376, off FM 473. These vineyards thrive in "downtown" Sisterdale, located between the East and West Sister Creeks. The winery, a restored cotton gin, produces traditional French wines. Weekday tours by appointment. Free. For information, call (210) 324-6704, or write: Rt. 2, P.O. Box 2481 C-1, Sisterdale, TX 78806.

Sisterdale General Store. FM 473. This historic general store and adjoining bar have served generations of customers. The bar sells Sister Creek Wine. Closed Monday. (210) 324-6767.

Day Trips from Austin

Welcome to Austin, the state capital and gateway to attractions in central Texas. With Austin as your base, you'll have a chance to visit both rugged hills to the west and miles of scenic roads and interesting small towns to the east. (For more information on Austin, see NORTHEAST FROM SAN ANTONIO, DAY TRIP 1.)

Austin is a high-tech city, with an economy based on computer-related industries and state government. The city of Austin takes in 485,000 residents, including a University of Texas population of over 50,000 students and faculty from around the world. This gives Austin an international feel, with many ethnic restaurants and specialty grocery stores. Many people have relocated here, attracted by the clean industry and beautiful weather.

Beyond the reach of Austin's bedroom communities, you'll find a Texas that's largely unchanged by the 1990s: bowling alleys still have pins set by hand; businesses close on Friday nights during high school football season; and pickup trucks seem to outnumber every other form of transportation. Some of the best barbecue in the world comes from the small towns that nestle in the hill country, a region so-called because of its rugged terrain. The topographical change represents the 1,800-mile Balcones Fault, which has separated the western hill country from the flat eastern farmland ever since a 3½-minute earthquake 30 million years ago.

This part of Texas gives you a chance to slow down, meet some local folks, and enjoy a good old-fashioned chicken-fried steak at the local diner.

For brochures and maps on Austin area attractions, call (800) 926-2282 or (512) 474-5171, or write: Austin Convention and Visitors Bureau, P.O. Box 2990, Austin, TX 78769.

DAY TRIPS
FROM AUSTIN

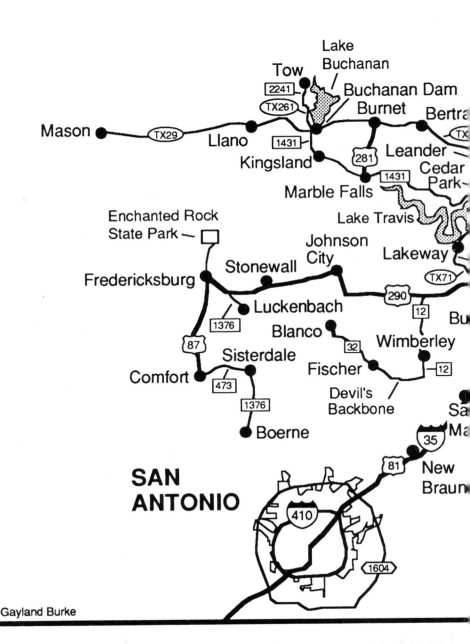

Gayland Burke

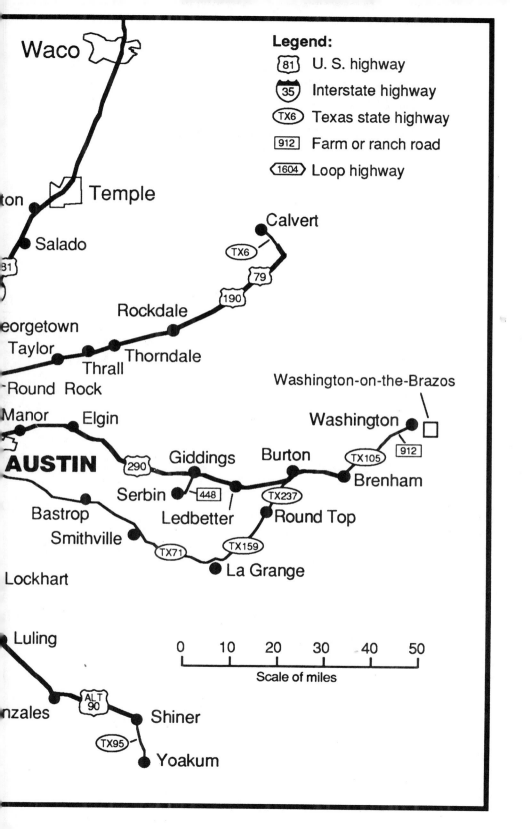

Day Trip 1

ROUND ROCK
GEORGETOWN
SALADO
BELTON
TEMPLE

ROUND ROCK

This Austin bedroom community located north on I-35 is named for the circular rock formation that lies in the middle of Brushy Creek.

Round Rock was the scene of a Wild West shoot-out a century ago. Sam Bass was a well-known outlaw in these parts back then, a stagecoach and train robber who boasted that he'd never killed a man. Bass planned to make his first bank robbery in Round Rock, but things went awry when the Texas Rangers learned his scheme. They were waiting as Bass and his gang rode into town on July 19, 1878, and they gravely wounded him during a gun battle in the 100 block of East Main Street. Bass fled from town and died two days later.

This colorful figure was buried in the old Round Rock cemetery, situated on what's now known as Sam Bass Road. The grave is near an interesting slave cemetery, a reminder of the cotton industry and plantation system that once dominated this area.

Round Rock was also once a part of the stagecoach route that stretched from Brownsville, Texas, to Helena, Arkansas. Frontiersmen used the round rock to judge the depth of Brushy Creek before crossing. Today visitors still can see coach tracks in the Brushy Creek riverbed, just west of I-35.

Every July Round Rock hosts Frontier Days, recalling its Wild West heritage with a reenactment of the Sam Bass shoot-out.

WHERE TO GO

Palm House Museum. 212 E. Main St. Built in the 1860s, this historic home now contains a two-room museum and the local Chamber of Commerce. In the kitchen and parlor hang photos and artifacts from Round Rock's early days. Look for the silver bowl whose lid was blown off during the Sam Bass shoot-out. Open daily. Free. (800) 747-3479 or (512) 255-5805.

WHERE TO EAT

Brushy Creek Inn. I-35 south, Taylor exit. Originally an 1860s home and now filled with antiques, this fine dining establishment and special occasion restaurant features Continental cuisine. Open for dinner only; call for hours and reservations. $$-$$$; []. (512) 255-2555.

El Matador. 113 W. Main St. This is the way Tex-Mex should be served, with chips and salsa brought to your table as soon as you sit down. The menu offers combinations galore and plates piled high with rice and beans, all at very reasonable prices. $; []. (512) 244-3030.

GEORGETOWN

Georgetown is an elegant community that rests on the border of farmland to the east and ranchland to the west. Located 10 miles north of Round Rock on I-35, this was once an active agricultural center. Today Georgetown is home to many Austin commuters and 1,200 students at Southwestern University, the oldest college in Texas.

Georgetown became a cattle center after the Civil War and the starting point of many northern cattle drives. The community grew in size but remained a small town into the late 1900s.

Austin's runaway growth during the 1980s eventually turned Georgetown into a bedroom community. Interstate 35 divides the city. To the west is "new" Georgetown, with many subdivisions along Williams Drive on the way to Lake Georgetown. "Old" Georgetown sits east of the highway, and among its main attractions are the winding North and South San Gabriel Rivers, which join together in shady San Gabriel Park.

Georgetown also participated in the Main Street Project, a joint program of the State Historical Commission and the National Trust for Historic Preservation. Take exit 261 off I-35 and continue right to Austin Avenue. Turn left at the light for a look at the restored courthouse square. With its stately oaks and shady lawn, it is so typical of Texas that it's been used as a set for several movies and TV shows.

WHERE TO GO

Georgetown History and Visitor Information Center. 101 W. Seventh St., on the square. Stop by for a copy of a Georgetown map, brochures on area attractions, and walking tour booklets and cassettes. The center also sells many Georgetown items, from posters to coffee cups. Open daily. (512) 863-5598.

Inner Space Caverns. West off I-35, exit 259. Discovered during the construction of the interstate, this cave is a cool getaway for summer travelers and was once a hideaway for animals as well. A skull of a peccary (a pig-like hoofed mammal) estimated to be a million years old has been found here, along with bones of a giant sloth and a mammoth. After reaching cave level aboard a small trolley, follow your guide for a tour of cave formations, a small lake, and evidence of those prehistoric visitors. Open daily. Fee. (512) 863-5545.

Mood Heritage Museum, Southwestern University. University Ave. (TX 29), east of Austin Ave. Located inside Southwestern University, a private Methodist college, this museum contains fossils, artifacts, and historical information and memorabilia relating to the Georgetown area and Southwestern University. Open Monday through Friday, closed during August and university holidays. Free. (512) 863-1997.

Lake Georgetown. Williams Dr. (FM 2338), west of Georgetown. This U.S. Army Corps of Engineers project offers swimming, fishing, boating, camping, and hiking opportunities. Free. (512) 863-3016.

WHERE TO SHOP

Georgetown presently has over a dozen antique shops. The Chamber of Commerce offers a free map of the shops listing hours and specialties. Call them at (512) 869-3545 for a copy or stop by the Visitors Center on the Square.

Georgetown Candle Factory. I-35 north, exit 259. This year-round factory produces thousands of varieties of hand-crafted candles, from classic tapers to popular snowball creations. Open daily. (512) 863-6025.

Texas Sampler. I-35 south, exit 262. Georgetown's largest antique shop is located in two connected homes that together offer 15 rooms of antiques and collectibles. Open daily. (512) 863-7694.

Georgetown Emporium. 114 E. Seventh St. Over 100 dealers in this antique mall sell everything from primitive furniture to estate jewelry. You'll also find the work of well-known Georgetown dollmaker Jan Hagara for sale here. Open daily. (512) 863-6845.

WHERE TO EAT

Walburg Restaurant. North from Georgetown on I-35 to exit 268; right four miles to Walburg. This restaurant is housed in the 1882 Walburg Mercantile building and features authentic German food and music. Behind the restaurant, a converted cotton gin serves as biergarten. The menu includes weinerschnitzel, bratwurst, sauerbraten, and some Texas favorites like chicken-fried steak and catfish. The restaurant hosts several annual celebrations, such as Harvestfest and Maifest. Closed Monday and Tuesday. Open for lunch and dinner Wednesday through Friday, dinner only on Saturday. $$; []. (512) 863-8440.

SALADO

Continuing north on I-35, Salado presents a shopping stop for interstate travelers. Antique stores, artists' galleries, and specialty shops fill the historic downtown buildings. *Salado* (pronounced "sa-LAY-dough") is a Spanish word meaning either salty or amusing, although residents prefer the latter interpretation.

This retirement community is located where Salado Creek flows beneath I-35. The site once was a stagecoach stop on the old Chisholm Trail and served the line that stretched from San Antonio to Little Rock.

Today the old rest stop has been converted to the modern Stagecoach Inn, located on the east side of I-35. Visitors' accommodations are found in a new addition, and the original building, where Sam Houston once delivered an anti-secession speech, is now an elegant restaurant.

The former stagecoach route, now called Main Street, is lined with historic structures housing antique shops and specialty stores. In all, 18 of these buildings are listed in the National Register of Historic Places, and 23 boast Texas historical markers.

WHERE TO GO

Central Texas Museum. Main St., across from Stagecoach Inn. This museum traces the history of the Salado area and all of the Brazos Trail—the rich farming area near the Brazos River. Open by appointment and during festivals. Fee. (817) 947-5232.

Pace Park. Downtown, off Main St. This beautiful area filled with tall oaks is an excellent spot to bring a picnic lunch and wade in the creek. Don't miss the statue of Sirena, located in the middle of the creek just behind the Grace Jones Shop (1 Royal Street). Local artist Troy Kelley sculpted the statue cast in bronze of the legendary Indian maiden who was transformed into a mermaid by a magical fish. Mornings you can see steam rising from the chilly waters of the pure springs near the statue. Free.

Driving Tape Tour. Prepared by the Bell County Historical Commission, this cassette tour directs you past 22 historic Salado sites. You'll see "driving tape tour" signs throughout town that correspond to an explanation on the cassette. Budget about two hours for the excursion, which explains the history and background behind each location. The tapes are available for rent at the Stagecoach Inn, Salado Galleries, and the Inn at Salado. Fee.

WHERE TO SHOP

Shopping is the main drawing card of Salado, and many stores are open daily. Most are expensive and sell one-of-a-kind, handmade items.

Salado Galleries. Main St., across from Stagecoach Inn. Fine art, including many paintings of central Texas bluebonnet fields, fill this gallery. Closed Monday. (817) 947-5110.

Salado Pottery. Beside the Stagecoach Inn. Here you'll find beautiful Salado-made pottery, from water pitchers to bird feeders. (817) 947-5935.

Royal Emporium of Salado. Main and Royal Sts. This store has a little bit of everything, from cowboy statues and teddy bears to Hoosier cabinets and delicate glassware. (817) 947-5718.

Shady Villa. Main St., across from Stagecoach Inn. This open-air mini-mall sells everything from unique kaleidoscopes and collectibles to Victorian jewelry and gifts from around the world. Most shops are open daily.

The Women's Exchange. N. Main St. at Salado Creek. Built in 1860, this structure has served as a drugstore, a law office, a stagecoach shop, and Salado's only saloon. Today it's filled with antiques and collectibles. (817) 947-5552.

Grace Jones Shop. One Royal St. You wouldn't expect to find the latest New York fashions in a Texas town of little more than 1,000 residents, but here it is. The store's owner, Grace Jones (not the actress), was once a fashion model. Open Monday through Saturday. (817) 947-5555.

Antique Jewelry and Collectibles. N. Main St. at Salado Creek. This is one of the most reasonably priced shops in town. Display cases are packed with old jewelry your grandmother might have owned. The place also sells a great deal of New Mexican Indian jewelry. (817) 947-9161.

Sir Wigglesworth. Rock Creek at Main St. Glass and ceramics, antique linens, baskets of every shape, and concrete animals from pigs to ducks are just a few of the items for sale in this crowded store. (817) 947-8846.

Fletcher's Books and Antiques. Main St. at Old Mill Rd. If you're looking for a Texas-related book, this is the place to go. Fletcher's has been in business for 60 years, 30 of those in Salado. The family-owned bookstore specializes in new, used and rare Texana books and also carries a selection of antiques. Open daily. (817) 947-5414.

WHERE TO STAY

Stagecoach Inn. I-35, east side. This reminder of Salado's early days started out as the Shady Villa Inn, an important rest stop on the Chisholm Trail. Today guests stay in a modern addition, and the original building, where Sam Houston once delivered an antisecession speech, has become an elegant restaurant. Notable guests have included George Armstrong Custer, Robert E. Lee, and outlaw Jesse James. $$; []. (817) 947-5111.

The Inn at Salado. N. Main St. at Pace Park. This lovely white two-story bed and breakfast is located in the main shopping district. Room rates include a full breakfast. $$; []. (817) 947-8200.

WHERE TO EAT

Stagecoach Inn. I-35, east side. This tony restaurant features waitresses who come to your table and recite the day's offerings by heart. Entrees include chicken-fried steak, baked ham, whole catfish, roast prime rib of beef, and T-bone steak. Don't miss the hush puppies or the banana fritters. Open daily for lunch and dinner. $$-$$$; []. (817) 947-5111.

BELTON

Continue north on I-35 to the town of Belton. Built on the Leon and Nolan Creeks, this community was once named Nolanville, a place where merchants sold goods from wagons and tin cups full of whiskey from a barrel.

Today Belton is a small town of 12,000 residents, best known as home of the University of Mary-Hardin Baylor. The Baptist college began here over a century ago and was once the women's school for Waco's Baylor University.

Two lakes, Stillhouse Hollow and the larger Belton Lake, lie outside the city limits. Both provide fishing, boating, camping, and a quiet retreat only a few minutes from busy I-35.

WHERE TO GO

Summer Fun USA. 1410 Waco Rd. This 6½-acre water theme park offers over 900 feet of water slides to help you cool off in the Texas heat. Hop on an inner tube and enjoy the 750-foot-long "Lazy River" ride or slide into the water from a 40-foot tower. There's a picnic area and concession area as well. Open seasonally. Fee. (817) 939-0366.

Stillhouse Hollow. US 190, four miles southwest of Belton. Six public parks envelope this lake. You'll find the most facilities at Stillhouse Park, the first you'll come to on US 190. Free. (817) 939-2461.

Belton Lake. TX 317, five miles northwest of Belton. Built on the Leon River, this winding 7,400-acre lake features 13 public parks within its 110 miles of shoreline. Trailer sites, camping, nature trails, and boat ramps are available. For information, call (817) 939-1829 or 939-0441, or write: Reservoir Manager, 99 FM 2271, Belton, TX 76513.

TEMPLE

The big sister to neighboring Belton, Temple is only a skip and a jump north on I-35. With over 45,000 residents, this city is the medical center for central Texas and an important industrial producer.

Temple was established by the Gulf, Colorado and Santa Fe Railroad and named for its chief construction engineer, B. M. Temple.

WHERE TO GO

Czech Heritage Museum. 520 N. Main St. The Czech people played an important role in settling central Texas, and their contribution is remembered in this museum housed in the SPJST (*Slovanska Podporujici Jednota Statu Texas,* or Slavonic Benevolent Order State of Texas) Insurance Company. The museum contains Czech costumes, a circa A.D. 1530 bible, quilts, a handmade dulcimer, and household items. Open weekdays during working hours. Free. (817) 773-1575.

Railroad and Pioneer Museum. South 31st St. at Ave. H. The old railroad depot once located in nearby Moody was transported here, boards, floor, and all. It's now open as a museum and library. Open afternoons, Tuesday through Saturday. Fee. (817) 778-6873.

ESPECIALLY FOR WINTER TEXANS

Outdoor America. East side of I-35 in Temple. If you're headed south, take exit 297, cross under I-35, and head north on the frontage road. If you traveling north on I-35, take exit 298. This shopping mall is dedicated to RVs, travel trailers, and fifth wheels. Although this is an authorized Winnebago center, it services all brands six days a week. With a scheduled appointment, you'll receive a free night of camping at the mall.

The retail stores carry parts and supplies for your vehicle as well as camping equipment, fitness items, and outdoor accessories. The mall sponsors several RV rallies annually, including the November annual Winter Texan Friendship Rally—four days of vendor exhibits, catered meals, and entertainment. Open daily. (817) 771-5466.

Day Trip 2
WACO

WACO

Located 106 miles north of Austin on I-35, this city of 100,000 is named for the Hueco Indians who resided here before the days of recorded history. The Hueco were attracted to this rich, fertile land at the confluence of the Brazos and Bosque Rivers.

Although Spanish explorers named this site "Waco Village" in 1542, over 300 years elapsed before permanent settlement began. At that time, Waco was part of the Wild West, with cattle drives, cowboys, and so many gunslingers that stagecoach drivers called the town "Six-Shooter Junction." (Drivers commonly asked passengers to strap on their guns before the stagecoach reached the rowdy community!)

In the 1870s Waco became a center of trade with the completion of a 474-foot suspension bridge across the Brazos, the longest inland river in Texas. The bridge still stands today, designed by the same engineers that constructed New York's Brooklyn Bridge years later.

Today Waco's Wild West heritage is tempered by a strong religious influence. The city is home to Baylor University, a Baptist liberal arts college of 11,000 students. The university has several excellent museums, open free to the public.

Some of the most scenic areas in Waco fall along the Brazos River. This waterway slices the city in half and provides miles of shoreline parks, shady walks, and downtown camping areas. The city is at work on a winding river walk to connect the suspension bridge at University Parks Drive with Fort Fisher on I-35.

WHERE TO GO

Fort Fisher Park. I-35 at exit 335B. This park was once the site of Fort Fisher, an outpost of the Texas Rangers built in 1837. The lawmen established a post here to protect the Brazos River crossing. Today the park contains the City of Waco Visitors Center, the Texas Rangers Hall of Fame, and a 35-acre campground with screened shelters on the riverbanks. Free. (817) 754-1433.

City of Waco Visitors Center. Fort Fisher. The visitors center provides helpful maps and brochures, and docents give advice on Waco attractions, accommodations, or restaurants. Open daily. Free. (800) WACO-FUN.

Texas Ranger Hall of Fame and Museum. Fort Fisher. If you're interested in the taming of Texas, budget a couple of hours for this large museum. Visitors here can see guns of every description used by the Rangers, who had the reputation of lone lawmen who always got their man. (The most famous Texas Ranger was the fictional Lone Ranger.) Dioramas in the Hall of Fame recount the early days of the Rangers, including their founding by Stephen F. Austin. A 20-minute slide show runs on the hour. Visit the James Michener Library, adjacent to the circular theater, for a look at the author's personal effects. Open daily. Free. (817) 754-1433.

Dr. Pepper Museum. 300 S. Fifth St. The famous Dr. Pepper soft drink was invented by pharmacist Dr. Charles Alderton at the Old Corner Drug Store in Waco, which once stood at Fourth Street and Austin Avenue. Today the drugstore is gone, but the original bottling plant remains open as a museum. Interesting exhibits and films offer a look at some early promotional materials as well as the manufacturing process of the unusual soft drink. (Also of note: the popular advertising slogan promoting Dr. Pepper as an energy booster to be consumed at "10-2-and 4.") After a look through the museum, visit the recreation of the Old Corner Drug Store fountain for an ice cream soda or (what else?) a Dr. Pepper. Fee. (817) 757-1024.

Armstrong-Browning Library. Eighth and Speight Sts., Baylor University campus. The works of Elizabeth Barrett Browning and husband Robert Browning fill this two-story library. The building also boasts the world's largest collection of secular stained glass windows, which illustrate the works of both writers (including Robert Browning's *The Pied Piper of Hamlin*). Take a guided tour to see the upstairs rooms furnished with the couple's belongings. Open daily except Sunday and some university holidays. Free. (817) 755-3566.

Strecker Museum. Sid Richardson Bldg., Baylor University campus. The oldest continually operating museum in Texas, this natural history collection includes displays on the rocks, fossils, and wildlife of Texas. Open daily. Free. (817) 755-1110.

Governor Bill and Vara Daniel Historic Village. Behind Fort Fisher at Canal St. and University Parks Dr. For a taste of Waco's days as "Six-Shooter Junction," visit this recreation of a 19th-century riverboat town. It holds a schoolhouse, a mercantile store, and, of course, a Wild West saloon. The buildings, once the property of Governor Daniel, were moved to this site from a plantation community in Liberty County, Texas, and restored by Baylor University. Open weekends only. Fee. (817) 755-1110.

Texas Sports Museum. University Parks Dr. and I-35. Waco's newest attraction is slated to open in summer 1992. Scheduled exhibits will include a baseball autographed by Texas Ranger Nolan Ryan, Earl Campbell's letter jacket, and Martina Navratilova's Wimbledon racket, as well as displays featuring prominent Texas high school athletes. Call for hours. Fee. (817) 756-2307.

Cameron Park. Brazos River at Herring Ave. This 368-acre municipal park is one of the largest in the state and holds Miss Nellie's Pretty Place, a beautiful wildflower garden filled with Texas bluebonnets. Free.

Central Texas Zoo. 19th St. to Airport Rd.; left to Monkey Run Rd. Waco presently is building a new habitat-friendly zoo scheduled to open in spring 1993. In the meantime, you can see interesting exhibits such as "Night World" (which features nocturnal animals), a snake house, and a children's petting zoo. Open daily. Fee. (817) 750-5976.

Suspension Bridge and Riverwalk. University Parks Dr., between Franklin and Washington Sts. Spanning the 800-mile-long Brazos River, this restored suspension bridge was once the longest in the world. Built in 1870, it eliminated the time-consuming process of having to cart cattle across the water by ferry. Today the structure is used as a pedestrian bridge bearing the motto "First across, still across." Open daily. Free.

The Art Center. 1300 College Dr. This exhibit hall and teaching center is located in the Mediterranean-style home of the late lumber magnate William Waldo Cameron. Exhibits here focus on Texas artists in all media. Open daily except Monday. Free. (817) 752-4371.

Historic Home Tours. Historic Waco Foundation, 810 Fourth St. Although a devastating tornado in 1953 destroyed many of Waco's historic structures, fortunately some still remain. Visitors see seven historic homes as well as the McLennan County Court House on this tour, all in the downtown area. One of the most interesting stops is "East Terrace," an Italianate villa on the east bank of the Brazos. Here guests once slept in unheated dormitories to discourage them from overstaying their welcome! Weekends only. Fee. (817) 753-5166.

WHERE TO EAT

Elite Cafe. On the circle at 2132 S. Valley Mills Dr. For years this popular restaurant advertised itself as "the place where the elite meet to eat." Today it's known for its '50s decor and homemade hamburger buns. Open for breakfast, lunch, and dinner. $$; []. (817) 754-4941.

Brazos Queen II. I-35 south, Fort Fisher exit. Anchored just below the I-35 bridge, this restaurant features steaks and seafood. It's popular with locals for special occasions. Dinner only; closed Sunday and Monday. $$-$$$; []. (817) 757-2332.

WHERE TO STAY

Quality Inn. 801 S. Fourth St., off I-35. The atrium in this two-story hotel encloses a swimming pool, a hot tub, and a restaurant $-$$; []. (817) 757-2000.

ESPECIALLY FOR WINTER TEXANS

Fort Fisher Park. I-35, exit 335B. Behind the City of Waco Visitors Center and the Texas Rangers Hall of Fame, you'll find a very nice 35-acre campground on the banks of the Brazos. This park makes a nice stopover for winter Texans on the way south. Campground office open daily. (800) 922-6386 or (817) 754-1433.

Day Trip 1

TAYLOR
THRALL
THORNDALE
ROCKDALE
CALVERT

TAYLOR

To reach Taylor, follow I-35 north into Round Rock (see NORTH FROM AUSTIN, DAY TRIP 1), then take the US 79 east exit and drive past the farming communities of Hutto and Frame Switch to Taylor. The route draws you through acres of cotton fields and blackland farms that stretch on for miles.

Taylor's claim to fame is its International Barbecue Cook-off in August and its controversial National Rattlesnake Sacking Championship and Roundup held every March. (See "Festivals and Celebrations" at the back of this book.)

Taylor was the hometown of former Texas governor Dan Moody as well as Bill Pickett, a black cowboy born in the area in 1860. Pickett originated the practice of "bulldogging"—throwing a bull by twisting his head until he falls. The well-known cowboy also had a habit of biting the steer's nose, a trick called "biting the bull" that he practiced on the rodeo circuit.

WHERE TO GO

Moody Museum. 114 W. Ninth St. Governor Dan Moody was born in this 1887 home, which today is filled with his furniture and personal belongings. He went to law school at the University of Texas, served in World War I, then returned to become governor at the age of 33. The hometown hero was best known for prosecuting members of the Ku Klux Klan in Williamson County. Open Sunday afternoon. Free. (512) 352-8654 or 352-5134.

Taylor Bedding Company. 400 Second St. This local success story began in 1903, when a local entrepreneur decided that he would rather sleep on home-grown cotton than corn-shuck mattresses. Taylor Bedding Company is now the home of Morning Glory Mattress. Call ahead to book a 30- to 45-minute tour of the plant and watch mattresses and box springs being produced. Tours Monday through Friday during working hours. Free. (800) 725-2333.

WHERE TO EAT

Mikeska's Barbecue. Left of US 79 as you enter town. This popular restaurant tempts diners with sausage, lamb ribs, pork ribs, ham, and baby back ribs. Open for lunch and dinner, Monday through Saturday, and lunch only on Sunday. $-$$; [] (American Express only). (512) 352-5561.

THRALL

When oil was discovered in 1915, Thrall's population skyrocketed as over 200 wells were drilled. As the saying goes, what goes up must come down, and Thrall was back on its way down as soon as oil production diminished. Today it's once again a quiet spot on US 79, composed of few blocks of homes than run parallel to the railroad.

WHERE TO GO

Stiles Farm Foundation. US 79, east of Thrall. This 3,200-acre demonstration farm is administered by Texas A & M University. Here new techniques are demonstrated to area farmers and ranchers. Visitors can take guided tours to see everything from hog raising to cotton growing. This is a great chance to have a look at an operating Texas farm and ranch. Call for appointment. Free. (512) 898-2214.

THORNDALE

Tiny Thorndale lies northeast of Thrall on US 79. It's another farming community built alongside the railroad tracks. As you drive through town, you can't miss the enormous cottonseed processing mill on the right, another of the many industries that make up this agricultural part of central Texas.

ROCKDALE

Unlike most of the other towns on this day trip, Rockdale is not known so much for farming but for what lies *beneath* the soil. This region is rich in lignite, a soft brown coal used as a fuel to generate electricity. The resulting energy in turn fuels Alcoa, America's largest aluminum-producing facility.

WHERE TO GO

Alcoa (Aluminum Company of America). Between Thorndale and Rockdale on US 79, look for roadside park sign "To Alcoa"; turn and follow signs to plant.

Alcoa, the largest smelter in North America, is not open to the public because of open flames and molten metal. Visitors, however, can take a drive-by tour of the facility, which is lit up like Christmas at night. The 24-hour operation has a 914-acre man-made lake and power plant on one side, and the smelter plant and mine on the other. (512) 446-8240.

CALVERT

To reach Calvert, continue northeast on US 79 to the intersection of US 190 in Hearne. Turn left and continue on US 190 (which becomes TX 6) to the town.

In 1868 Calvert was the end of the line for the Houston and Central Railway. With over 10,000 residents, it was the fourth largest city in the state. P. C. Gibson, a cotton trader, came to the area and built the world's largest cotton gin in the 1870s. A 1965 fire and a tornado a decade later all but demolished the once-grand business.

One of Calvert's most colorful figures was Myra Bell Shirley, better known as Belle Starr. Some say that Shirley was a Confederate spy; others say she befriended outlaws like Jesse James. Belle Starr's demise is the stuff of legend: She was either shot in the back by her Indian lover, Sam Starr, or hanged for stealing horses. No one knows for sure.

Calvert's boom town status faded when the railroad was extended to Dallas. Things stayed quiet in Calvert for many years, but because of its many Victorian homes and refurbished downtown businesses, the town was declared a National Historic District in 1978. Today Calvert calls itself "The Antique Center of Texas," and several shops along Main Street offer buyers a nice selection of collectibles.

WHERE TO SHOP

Boll Weevil. 506 Main St. This fine antique shop specializes in 18th- and 19th-century furniture and porcelain. Open Wednesday through Monday. (409) 364-2835.

Memory Lane Antique Mall. 406 Main St. This two-story, multidealer mall is filled with furniture, collectibles, and linens. Don't miss the old elevator inside, located near the bargain floor. Open daily. (409) 364-2889.

Milly's Antiques. 602 Main St. This antique shop has a little of everything, including a wide selection of glassware. The owner has a special interest in marbles, and even the most cherished items in his collection are for sale. Open daily. (817) 746-7890.

S & S Antiques. 517 Main St. Primitives, Raggedy Ann dolls, lunch boxes, and antique linens are just a few of the offerings browsers find in this shop. Closed Tuesday and Wednesday. (409) 364-2634 or 364-2752.

WHERE TO STAY

Our House Bed and Breakfast. 406 E. Texas St. This two-story, 5,000-square-foot home once was the residence of P. C. Gibson, the owner of the world's largest cotton gin. The home's five elegant guest rooms share two baths. Children are permitted, but smoking is not. Rates include a full breakfast. $$; no []. (409) 364-2909.

Day Trip 1

MANOR
ELGIN
SERBIN
LEDBETTER
BURTON
BRENHAM
WASHINGTON-ON-THE-BRAZOS

MANOR

To reach Manor, drive east from Austin on US 290. This community was a quiet suburb until a few years ago, when Texas legalized pari-mutuel wagering. Today the town is home to Manor Downs, a quarterhorse track, with fall races from September through December and a spring season starting in February. Races are held on Friday, Saturday, and Sunday afternoons. Fee. For race times, call (512) 272-4042.

ELGIN

Continue east from Manor on US 290 to Elgin. This small town enjoys star status because of Elgin sausage, a spicy concoction that's sold throughout this part of the state.

WHERE TO EAT

Southside Market. 1212 US 290 W. This casual barbecue eatery has been the source of Elgin sausage since 1882. The back dining room is filled with Formica tables, the smell of smoke, and happy customers. Open for lunch, early dinner, and takeout. Closed Sunday. $; no []. (512) 285-3407.

SERBIN

From Elgin, continue east on US 290 for 29 miles to Giddings. Turn south on US 77, then south again on FM 448 for five miles. At the intersection of FM 2239, turn right and continue two miles to the hamlet of Serbin.

This town was settled by the Wends, Germans of Slavic descent who came to Texas in the 1850s and brought with them the Gothic architecture of their homeland. From 1865 to 1890 this was a thriving town, boasting dry goods, jewelry, drug, and music stores, three doctors, and two dentists. When Serbin was bypassed by the railroad, it quickly declined.

WHERE TO GO

St. Paul Lutheran Church. Off FM 2239. The historic St. Paul Lutheran Church, a smaller version of the elaborate German cathedrals of the 18th and 19th centuries, was built in 1859 of native sandstone. To replicate marble, the parishioners painted the plaster walls with turkey feather brushes. This church once had a very unusual seating arrangement: Men sat in the balcony across from the pulpit, women and children took the pews on the floor. Open daily. Free. (409) 366-2219.

Texas Wendish Heritage Museum. Off FM 2239, near St. Paul Lutheran Church. You'll find antique furniture and household items as well as photos of the early days in this local history museum. Open afternoons, Sunday through Friday. Fee; students free. (409) 366-2441.

LEDBETTER

To continue on this day trip, retrace your steps back to Giddings and US 290. Drive east on US 290 for nine miles to the tiny community of Ledbetter. Once the first town in the county to boast a railroad, its importance declined when nearby La Grange became a freight center.

WHERE TO GO

Stuermer Store. South side of US 290. This metal building has served as a general store since 1870. At one time, the current owner's grandfather ran a saloon next door. Now the businesses are joined to create a general store, museum, and soda shop all in one. A working museum exhibits the tools of the early grocery, from cheese cutters to coffee grinders. Today the wildest drink in the old saloon is an old-fashioned malt. You can order up some local Blue Bell ice cream or fresh sandwiches at the fountain, and listen to a free tune on a jukebox packed with oldies. Open Monday through Saturday. Free. (409) 249-3330.

BURTON

Follow US 290 east past the tiny town of Carmine, which is full of antique shops (open Saturday only), to the tiny agricultural community of Burton, located just off US 290 on FM 390. With a population of slightly more than 300, this town has a surprising number of shops and businesses, many open only on weekends.

Take some time to walk around the historic buildings and drop in the Burton Mercantile. Here you can make arrangements for a guide to take you on a tour of the restored gin, railroad depot, and caboose.

WHERE TO GO

Burton Cotton Gin. Main St., across from Burton Mercantile. Stop in the mercantile to arrange for a 45-minute tour of this restored gin, a National Historic Landmark. You'll see the engine room, the mechanical floor, the ginning floor, and an old cobbler shop where harnesses were made for the horses that pulled in the cotton wagons. Tours also can be conducted in German. Open on a walk-in basis. Fee. (409) 289-2863 or 289-3846.

BRENHAM

Return to US 290 and continue east to Brenham. In this state, Brenham means the Blue Bell Creamery. This is one of the biggest independent manufacturers of ice cream in the country, selling over 25 million half-gallon containers a year. It's as Texan as bluebonnets and two-stepping, and expatriates have been known to carry back picnic freezers full of Brenham's product.

Brenham has a host of other, less fattening attractions as well, including a historic downtown that's filled with antique and specialty shops, and residential streets that showcase splendid antebellum and Victorian homes.

A free brochure of historic sites is available from the Washington County Chamber of Commerce, 314 S. Austin in Brenham, or by calling (409) 836-3695.

WHERE TO GO

Blue Bell Creamery. FM 566 off US 290 west. Blue Bell has been making ice cream since 1911, when they packaged their product in wooden tubs and delivered it by horse-drawn wagon. The "tasting room" here is a turn-of-the-century-style soda shop, where visitors can choose from among 25 flavors. After a free dish of your personal favorite, you can have a look around the Country Store, which sells everything from strawberry-ice-cream-scented pencils to piggy banks in the shape of the company's early delivery trucks. Open daily. Tours conducted Monday through Friday only; call for times. Fee. (800) 327-8135.

Monastery of St. Clare Miniature Horse Ranch. TX 105, nine miles northeast of Brenham. This monastery is occupied by a group of Catholic nuns who raise miniature horses to support themselves. The tiny horses, some less than 34 inches tall, sell for anywhere from $3,000 to $30,000. On self-guided tours visitors see the barn and grooming facilities (with miniature carriages and harnesses) and the Mini Mansion where the horses are reared. The Art Barn is filled with thousands of ceramics made by the nuns, including tiny reproductions of the horses. Open 2-4 p.m. daily. Free. (409) 836-9652.

Ellison's Greenhouses. Horton and Stone Sts., south of Blue Bell Creamery on Loop 577. Ellison's produces African violets, Easter lilies, mums, tulips, and many other decorative flowers. Every year they grow 250,000 poinsettia cuttings and 80,000 finished poinsettias, some of which find their way to the State Capitol and Governor's Mansion. Open to the public Friday and Saturday. Free. (409) 836-6011.

Antique Carousel at Fireman's Park. From Main St., take Austin Pkwy. north to Academy St. The antique carousel is located inside Fireman's Park, a popular picnic spot shaded by tall post oaks. Housed in a round building, the carousel is available for group tours and special occasions. Built before 1910 by the Hershell-Spillman Company of New York, this is one of few carousels to be constructed for a traveling carnival. Group tours include a free ride. For information, call (409) 836-7911.

WHERE TO EAT

Bluebonnet Hills Grill and Garden. 3955 Bluebonnet Hills Blvd., US 290 east of Brenham. This large restaurant features country foods served family style with a choice of meats and vegetables. A Sunday buffet offers fresh seafood. Open for dinner Wednesday through Saturday, lunch only on Sunday. $$; []. (409) 836-4642.

WHERE TO STAY

The Brenham area is home to nearly a dozen bed and breakfasts, many located in historic homes or on local farms. The city also provides lodging in several motels. For more information on accommodations, obtain free copies of the "Washington County Bed and Breakfast Guide" and the "Lodging Guide" by writing: Washington County Convention and Visitor Bureau, 314 S. Austin, Brenham, TX 77833.

James Walker Homestead. Old Chappell Hill Rd., a few miles east of Brenham. This structure was built in 1826 as the home of James Walker, one of the first 300 colonists who came to Texas with Stephen F. Austin. Today the original log construction is still visible inside the home, which is furnished with Texas antiques. The bed and breakfast does not accommodate children, and no smoking is permitted in the house. Lodging includes two double bedrooms and a single bedroom. $$$; no [] . (409) 836-6717.

WASHINGTON-ON-THE-BRAZOS

To reach this community, alternately called Washington and Washington-on-the-Brazos, take TX 105 northeast of Brenham for 14 miles, then turn right on FM 912.

This town dates back to the days of a ferry landing on the Brazos River that operated at the site from 1822. Washington has become best known, however, as the birthplace of the republic of Texas. On a cold March day in 1836, founders gathered here and signed the Declaration of Independence, establishing Texas as a separate country.

From 1842 to 1845, this town served as the capital of the republic, also gradually becoming a commerce center on the busy Brazos. Thus, when the seat of government was moved to Austin, Washington hung on, kept alive by its position on the river. Eventually, though, in the 1850s, Washington was by-passed by the railroads, and the community dwindled to a tiny dot on the map.

WHERE TO GO

Washington-on-the-Brazos State Historical Park. Located on the banks of the Brazos, this quiet park is·shaded by acres of walnut and pecan trees. This is a day-use park only, with picnic tables along the river, and admission is free. Its three main sections include the following points of interest:

Independence Hall. The original building where the signing of the Texas Declaration of Independence took place did not survive the 19th century. In 1901 a group of citizens erected a monument at the site. The simple frame building reconstructed here holds long, mismatched tables and unadorned chairs. Open daily. Free.

Barrington. This was once the home of Anson Jones, the fourth and last president of the Republic of Texas. Open daily March through August; weekends only September through February. Fee. (409) 878-2214.

Star of the Republic Museum. Built in the shape of the Lone Star State, this museum covers the republic period. Visitors can start with a 20-minute film narrated by Bill Moyers for an overview of the period. Upstairs, exhibits cover all aspects of commerce during the 19th century, including displays on the general store, blacksmithing, steamboats, and carpentry. Open daily March through August; Wednesday through Sunday remainder of the year. Free. (409) 878-2461.

Day Trip 1

BASTROP
SMITHVILLE
LA GRANGE
ROUND TOP

BASTROP

To reach Bastrop, take TX 71 southeast from Austin. Unlike the juniper-dotted hills to the west or the rolling farmland to the east, the Bastrop area is surrounded by a pine forest called Lost Pines. Here grows the westernmost stand of loblolly pines in America. Scientists believe that these trees were once part of the forests of East Texas, but climactic changes over the last 10,000 years account for the farmland now separating the Lost Pines from their cousins to the east.

Bastrop is a popular day trip for Austinites looking for a chance to shop and savor some quiet country life in a historic setting.

WHERE TO GO

Walking Tour of Historic Bastrop. Visitor Information kiosk, Main and Spring Sts. Pick up a copy of this brochure for information about the town's 30 historic structures. Free. (512) 321-2419.

Lock's Drug. 1003 Main St. This turn-of-the-century drugstore features an antique mirrored fountain where you can belly up for a thick, creamy malt. Built-in cabinets are still labeled with the names of their original contents, and old apothecary tools still sit in the front windows. Closed Sunday. (512) 321-2551.

Bastrop County Historical Society Museum. 702 Main St. This 1850 frame cabin contains Indian relics and pioneer exhibits. Open Saturday and Sunday afternoons. Fee. (512) 321-6177.

Bastrop State Park. TX 21, 1½ miles east of Bastrop. Beautiful piney woods are the main draw at this 3,500-acre park, where facilities include a nine-hole golf course, campsites, and a 10-acre fishing lake. The 1930s-built stone and cedar cabins are very popular and should be booked well in advance. They feature fireplaces, bathrooms, and kitchen facilities. Fee to enter park. For reservations, call (512) 321-2101, or write: P.O. Box 518, Bastrop, TX 78602.

Central Texas Museum of Automotive History. South on FM 304 to FM 535; left one mile to Rosanky. This private museum is dedicated to the collection and preservation of old cars and accessories. The vehicles on display include a 1935 Rolls-Royce Phantom, a La France fire engine, and a 1922 Franklin. Open Wednesday through Sunday, April through September; Friday through Sunday remainder of the year. Fee. (512) 237-2051 or 237-2635.

WHERE TO SHOP

Park your car and enjoy an afternoon of browsing through the many antique and specialty stores along Main Street.

Tejas Galleria. 932 Main St. Navajo and Zuni jewelry, Cherokee moccasins, and Peruvian wall hangings are just a few of the items in this eclectic Southwestern shop. Open daily. (512) 321-1881.

Pine Cottage. 913 Main St. This store features the works of many area artists, including some beautiful clay hummingbird feeders. Open Tuesday through Saturday. (512) 321-4121.

WHERE TO EAT

Bastrop BBQ and Meat Market. 919 Main St. This old-fashioned Texas barbecue joint has a meat market up front and a dining room in the back. Sausage, beef brisket, and chicken are the order of the day, served with sides of beans and potato salad. Open for lunch and dinner. Closed Sunday. $; no []. (512) 321-7719.

WHERE TO STAY

The Colony Bed and Breakfast Inn. 707 Pine St., one block off Main St. This beautiful bed and breakfast is housed behind the owner's antique shop. You can select from two accommodations: an antique-filled room with use of a shady courtyard, or a historic cabin with a large front porch. Both rooms include a full breakfast and a complimentary bottle of champagne. $$; no []. (512) 321-7984.

SMITHVILLE

Continue east from Bastrop on TX 71 to Smithville, a small town that's built alongside the railroad tracks at the edge of the piney woods and home of Buescher State Park. En route you may want to make a quick stop in Alum Creek, a small community located on TX 71 between Bastrop and Smithville. The former site of a fort and a stagecoach stop, Alum Creek is now best known for its antique and junk shops located on the north side of TX 71.

Smithville was once a riverboat ferry stop on the Colorado River. In the 1880s, the railroad replaced the ferries as the main mode of transportation, and tracks were laid across town. Today the railroad still plays an important part in Smithville's economy.

WHERE TO GO

Smithville Railroad Historical Park. 100 W. First St. Built beside the tracks, this new park has two cabooses and a depot relocated here from West Point, a community east of town. The Chamber of Commerce office is housed in the depot as well. Open weekdays. Free. (512) 237-2313.

Buescher State Park. Three miles north of town, via TX 71 and FM 2104, or access from Park Road 1. This park is home to loblolly pines, a 30-acre lake, hardwood trees, migrating birds, and even an occasional flying squirrel. Visitors can enjoy ample campsites and screened shelters, as well as a playground and picnic area. Fee. (512). 237-2241.

Smithville Heritage Museum. 602 Main St. This 1908 home contains the Smithville archives and a museum of local memorabilia. Open Tuesday. Free. (512) 237-4545.

LA GRANGE

Four miles southeast of Smithville on the left side of TX 71 is a scenic overlook, an excellent place to pull over for a picnic. While you're here you can gaze at the miles of rolling hills and farmland that attracted many German and Czech immigrants a century ago.

Continue on TX 71 to the infamous community of La Grange. For generations this was a quiet town in the center of a farming region. In the 1970s, however, La Grange caught the attention of the public with the unveiling of the Chicken Ranch, a brothel that became the subject of the Broadway musical and movie, *The Best Little Whorehouse in Texas*. Today the Chicken Ranch is gone, but La Grange still has other sights to see.

WHERE TO GO

Monument Hill/Kreische Brewery State Historic Site. US 77, one mile south of La Grange. Located on a bluff high above town, this site is the home to two combined parks.

Monument Hill Historical Park is the burial site for the Texans who died in the Dawson Massacre and the Mier Expedition, two historic Mexican conflicts that occurred in 1842, six years after the Texas Revolution. The Dawson Massacre took place near San Antonio when La Grange citizen Nicholas Dawson gathered Texans to halt the continual Mexican attacks. Dawson's men were met by hundreds of Mexican troops and 35 Texans were killed.

The Mexican village of Mier was attacked in a retaliatory move, resulting in the capture of Texas soldiers and citizens by Mexican General Santa Anna, who ordered every 10th man to be killed. The Texans were blindfolded and forced to draw beans: 159 of them white and 17 black. Men who drew white beans were imprisoned; those who drew black ones were executed.

The Kreische Brewery State Historical Site recalls a far more cheerful time in Texas history. Heinreich Kreische was a German who immigrated here from Europe. In 1849 he purchased the hilltop and the adjoining land, including the burial ground of those Texas heroes, for his brewery site. Eventually he became the third largest beer producer in the state, opening one of the first breweries in Texas.

Open daily until 5 p.m. Guided tours of the brewery ruins run on weekends. Fee (one admission covers both adjacent sites). (409) 968-5658.

Hermes Drug Store. 148 N. Washington St. Established in 1856, this is the oldest drugstore in continuous operation in Texas. Visitors can see authentic old-time structures, beveled mirrors, and more. Open Monday through Saturday. (409) 968-5835.

WHERE TO EAT

Bon Ton Restaurant. Old TX 71. This combination restaurant and bakery is always busy with locals and travelers who've heard of the Bon Ton's reputation for good home cooking. This is the best of Texas foods—chicken-fried steak, fried chicken, mashed potatoes, fried okra, and fresh rolls. There are daily specials, plus a popular buffet. Don't miss the homemade kolaches and bread. Open daily for breakfast, lunch, and dinner. $; []. (409) 968-5863.

ROUND TOP

Drive northeast on TX 159 to TX 237, then turn north and continue on to Round Top, a favorite stop with history buffs. Officially founded in 1835 by settlers from Stephen F. Austin's second colony, this town is filled with restored homes, log cabins, and country stores.

Round Top is also home to a world-class music and theater facility. Festival Hill, located just outside of town, offers visiting symphony orchestras and Shakespearean performances under the summer stars.

WHERE TO GO

Henkel Square. TX 237, on the town square. This is one of the finest restorations of pioneer buildings in the state, with an apothecary shop, schoolhouse, church, and homes dating from 1820 to 1879. Guides lead visitors on a tour of the structures, pointing out the tinted walls of the log cabin, the outdoor staircase in the Henkel house (typical in many German homes), and the elaborately stenciled ceiling. Open afternoons daily. Fee. (713) 249-3308.

Winedale Historical Center. Four miles east of Round Top via FM 1457;

north on FM 2714. Winedale is administered by the University of Texas at Austin for the study of central Texas ethnic cultures. The center consists of a Visitors Center and the McGregor-Grimm House, a two-story Greek revival farmhouse built by a planter in 1861. Guided tours point out the decorative wall paintings, a luxury in this area at the time. Open weekends. Fee. (409) 278-3530.

Festival Hill. TX 237, five blocks north of Henkel Square. This music and theater center was founded by noted pianist James Dick. During the school year, Festival Hill presents monthly concerts. In the summer, the center hosts students from around the world who entertain guests with musical performances and Shakespearean productions. The center is housed in historic buildings, including an 1870 farmhouse and a former black school. Fee. (409) 249-3129.

Day Trip 1

LOCKHART
LULING
GONZALES
SHINER
YOAKUM

LOCKHART

Lockhart is a conglomeration of the stuff of Texas legends: Indian battles, cattle drives, cotton, and oil. This small town, located 23 miles south of Austin on US 183, contains a state park and lots of history.

The biggest event in Lockhart's past was the Battle of Plum Creek in 1840. Over 600 Comanches raided the community of Linnville and were on their way home when they passed through this area. A group of settlers joined forces with the Tonkowa Indians to attack the Comanches, driving the Indians further west and ending the Indian attacks in the region. This battle is reenacted every May at the Chisholm Trail Roundup.

Lockhart is also well known as the home of Mebane cotton. Developed by A. D. Mebane, this strain is resistant to the boll weevil, an insect that can demolish not only whole fields but entire economies as well.

WHERE TO GO

Lockhart State Park. FM 20, west of town. This 263-acre park has a nine-hole golf course, fishing on Plum Creek, picnic areas, a swimming pool, and campsites for both tents and trailers. Many of the facilities were built by the Civilian Conservation Corps in the 1930s. Open daily. Fee. For camping reservations, call (512) 398-3479, or write: Rt. 3, P.O. Box 69, Lockhart, TX 78644.

Dr. Eugene Clark Library. 217 S. Main St. Built in 1889, this is the oldest continually operating library in Texas. Modeled after the Villa Rotunda in Vicenza, Italy, it has stained glass windows, ornate fixtures, and a stage where President William Taft once spoke. Open Monday through Saturday. Free. (512) 398-3223.

WHERE TO EAT

Kreuz Market. 208 S. Commerce St. Vegetarians, head elsewhere. This barbecue restaurant is a meat-only kind of place, offering spicy sausage, pork loin, prime rib, and pork ribs, all served in an atmosphere that's little changed since the present owner took over in 1948. The meat market's up front for take-out orders; the dining area is in the back. The two are connected by a smoke-filled hallway and dinner counter. Open daily, early morning to evening. $-$$; no []. (512) 398-2361.

Black's Barbecue. 215 N. Main St. This cafeteria-style restaurant is reputedly the oldest barbecue joint in Texas under the same continual ownership. Beef brisket is the specialty of the house, along with sausage, ribs, chicken, and ham. There's also a fully stocked salad bar. Open daily for lunch and dinner. $-$$; no []. (512) 398-2712.

LULING

Continue south on US 183 for 17 miles to Luling, an oil center that's still alive with pumping wells. Many of the pumpjacks are decorated as cartoon characters. (For more about Luling, read EAST FROM SAN ANTONIO, DAY TRIP 1.)

GONZALES

Continue south on US 183 for 13 miles to Gonzales, one of Texas's most historic cities. This is the "Come and Take It" town where the Texas Revolution began in 1835. (Read about this skirmish and the many attractions in Gonzales in EAST FROM SAN ANTONIO, DAY TRIP 2.)

SHINER

Take US 90A east of Gonzales for 32 miles to the tiny town of Shiner, best known as the home of Shiner beer. If you make the trip during the week, stop by for a free tour and a sample of the hometown product. (For information on the brewery and other Shiner attractions, see EAST FROM SAN ANTONIO, DAY TRIP 2.)

YOAKUM

From Shiner, drive south on TX 95 for eight miles to US 77A. Turn right and continue for two more miles. Yoakum is home to 11 leather companies, and thus is nicknamed "The Leather Capital of the World." Guided tours of these leather factories can be arranged. (See EAST FROM SAN ANTONIO, DAY TRIP 2.)

Day Trip 2

BUDA
SAN MARCOS

BUDA

Head south from Austin on I-35 to the small town of Buda, located on Loop 4 to the west of the highway. This sleepy railroad town is a busy spot on weekends, when shoppers come to hunt antiques. (See NORTHEAST FROM SAN ANTONIO, DAY TRIP 2.)

SAN MARCOS

Continue south on I-35 to San Marcos, the home of Southwest Texas State University, two amusement parks, and the crystal-clear San Marcos River. (See NORTHEAST FROM SAN ANTONIO, DAY TRIP 2.)

Day Trip 1
SAN ANTONIO

SAN ANTONIO

As Texas's third largest city, San Antonio has the reputation of a fun-loving town. Located 80 miles south of Austin on I-35, the city always has something going on to attract visitors. No matter when you choose to visit, you can bet that somebody, somewhere is hosting a festival. Perhaps it has something to do with the sunshine or the fresh air. Whatever it is, you can feel it. It sizzles up like fajitas out of the city's Hispanic heritage, which abounds with colorful tradition and vivid memories.

San Antonio's rich cultural past dates back to the early Indians who settled the area. They were followed by the 17th-century Spaniards, who came here in search of wealth. Later a group of Franciscan friars established a chain of missions designed to convert the Indians of the Southwest to Christianity. In 1718 Mission San Antonio de Valera, better known as the Alamo, became the first of five such structures in the city.

Except for the Alamo, the missions are found in the San Antonio Missions National Historic Park, located within the city limits. The National Park Service has assigned interpretive themes to each of the four—the active parish churches of Mission Concepción, Mission San Juan Capistrano, Mission San Francisco de la Espada, and Mission San Jose. The latter, established in 1720, hosts a colorful "Mariachi Mass" each Sunday at noon.

San Antonio is also a foodie's paradise. This is the city that heralded the birth of *fajitas*—strips of marinated charcoal-grilled skirt steak. Here you'll also find to-die-for guacamole, *pico de gallo* (a Mexican condiment of spiced raw vegetables), and fresh flour tortillas.

With two excellent theme parks, a world-class zoo, and wonderful museums, San Antonio offers much more to see and do than this book can possibly list. For a complete rundown of possibilities, contact the San Antonio Convention and Visitors Bureau (call 800-447-3372, or write: P.O. Box 2277, San Antonio, TX 78298) or stop in the Visitors Center at Alamo Plaza (across from the Alamo), where you also can pick up information on the VIA streetcars that connect major tourist sites. The Center is open daily. (210) 299-8155.

DOWNTOWN: RIVER WALK AREA

The River Walk stretches for several miles from South St. Mary's Street to Alamo Street, and along Crockett and Market Streets. The Paseo del Rio, as it's also called, is a European-style river walk that lies below street level. Part of an urban renovation project five decades ago, the River Walk is now a top San Antonio attraction. Its winding sidewalks, which follow an arm of the San Antonio River, are lined with two-story specialty shops, sidewalk cafes, luxury hotels, art galleries, and bars. Like New Orleans's Bourbon Street, this area of San Antonio has an atmosphere all its own. Sidewalk bars sell potent frozen margaritas for visitors to sip as they stroll the winding pathway. Arched bridges connect the two sides of the walk, so visitors never have to venture up to street level.

One of the busiest sections of the Paseo del Rio extends from the Hyatt Regency San Antonio at Crockett Street to the Hilton Hotel at Market Street. This stretch of walk boasts most of the sidewalk restaurants and shops. From Commerce Street you can head up to the Convention Center and the Rivercenter Mall. This part of the walk includes a waterfall, lush greenery, and a more tranquil atmosphere than the dining and shopping areas.

WHERE TO GO

The Alamo. Alamo Plaza, between Houston and Crockett Sts. Located in the very heart of San Antonio, the Alamo was once surrounded on all sides by the forces of Mexican General Santa Anna. Now it's enveloped by high-rise office structures and a central plaza.

This "Cradle of Texas Liberty," situated on the east side of Alamo Plaza, is probably the most famous spot in Texas. Established in 1718 as the Mission San Antonio de Valero, it plunged into history on March 6, 1836, when 188 men died after being attacked by the Mexican forces of General Santa Anna. Among the most famous defenders were Jim Bowie, William B. Travis, and Davy Crockett.

Symbol of the state's independence and courage, the Alamo draws continuous crowds throughout the year. Visitors entering the main building, the Shrine, can see exhibits such as Bowie's famous knife and Davy Crockett's rifle, "Old Betsy." Those interested also can take a self-guided tour of the museum, the Long Barracks, and the beautiful courtyard. Open daily. Free. (210) 225-1391.

River Taxis. River Walk at Commerce St., across from Hilton Hotel and Rivercenter Mall. One of the most pleasurable and least expensive attractions in town, these open barges take passengers on 40-minute narrated cruises through the heart of San Antonio from morning until late evening. Special dinner candlelight cruises afford a romantic look at the city by night. Open daily. Fee. (210) 222-1701.

Tower of the Americas. HemisFair Park. This 750-foot tower is topped by a rotating restaurant that serves lunch and dinner. An observation deck offers an unbeatable view of the city. Open daily. Fee. (210) 299-8617.

Institute of Texan Cultures. HemisFair Park. This fascinating museum features exhibits and a multimedia presentation showcasing the 26 different ethnic groups who came here from around the world to settle the new frontier called Texas. Open Tuesday through Sunday. Free. (210) 266-7651.

IMAX Theater. Rivercenter Mall. This theater features *The Price of Freedom*, a 45-minute movie about the battle of the Alamo. The six-story screen and six-channel sound immerses you in the glory of the struggle, and it's a good thing to see before visiting the historic site. The theater alternates this movie with other IMAX features, so call for show times. Open daily. Fee. (210) 225-IMAX.

Hertzberg Circus Collection and Museum. 210 Market St. One of the largest circusiana collections in the world, this unusual museum contains more than 20,000 items of big top memorabilia, including antique circus posters, Tom Thumb's miniature carriage, and a scale model of a three-ring circus. Open Monday through Saturday, October through April; daily May through September. Fee. (210) 299-7810.

Steves Homestead. 509 King William St. This grand home was built in 1876 and is currently the only one in the elegant King William Historic District that is open to the public. The Victorian mansion's interior is filled with original furniture, and the grounds include several antique carriages and the gardener's quarters, now a visitors center. Open daily. Fee. (210) 225-5924.

Plaza Theatre of Wax. 301 Alamo Plaza. This attraction has wax figure displays of movie and TV celebrities as well as a theater of horrors. The Heroes of the Lone Star section is interesting, with realistic scenes depicting the fall of the Alamo. Ripley's Believe it or Not is located in the same building, and you can buy separate or combination tickets to the two attractions. Open daily. Fee. (210) 224-9299.

WHERE TO SHOP

La Villita. Exit through Hilton Hotel, one block right on South Alamo St. This area on the east bank of the San Antonio River was developed in the mid-to-late 18th century by Mexican settlers who lived, without land title, on the outskirts of the Alamo mission.

Today La Villita is San Antonio's finest crafts area, filled with weavers, glassblowers, sculptors, and even boot makers. Within the restored buildings shops sell everything from woven wall hangings to silver jewelry, and the historic Little Church is often the site of weddings. Most shops open daily. Free.

Rivercenter Mall. Bounded by Commerce, Bowie, Crockett, and Alamo Sts. This three-story mall is home to several anchor stores as well as specialty shops and restaurants. On the enclosed bridge over the river vendors sell crafts and specialty items. The River Walk makes a U-turn in an outdoor dining area. Two hours free parking. Open daily. (210) 225-0000.

WHERE TO EAT

Casa Rio. 430 Commerce St. Open for nearly half a century, this popular Tex-Mex restaurant was one of the first businesses along the river. Patrons can sit at the colorful umbrella-shaded tables on the river's edge and enjoy enchiladas, tacos, and other typical regional fare. There's also indoor dining for chilly evenings. Open for lunch and dinner. $; []. (210) 225-6718.

WHERE TO STAY

Hyatt Regency San Antonio. 123 Losoya St. This beautiful hotel, with its open atrium and glass elevators, is located directly on the River Walk. A stream flows through the hotel outside to the River Walk, where an open-air jazz bar provides nightly entertainment. $$$; []. (800) 233-1234 or (210) 222-1234.

Emily Morgan Hotel. 705 E. Houston St., next to the Alamo. General Santa Anna was enamored with a mulatto slave named Emily Morgan, who acted as a spy for the Texas army. Thanks in part to her efforts, Sam Houston's troops defeated Santa Anna's men at San Jacinto on April 21, 1836, winning the Texas Revolution. Emily Morgan came to be known as "The Yellow Rose of Texas," the namesake of a famous song as well as this 177-room hotel. The rooms overlook the Alamo courtyard or Alamo Plaza, and all have Jacuzzis. $$; []. (800) 824-6674.

DOWNTOWN: MARKET SQUARE

Colorful Market Square, bounded by San Saba, Santa Rosa, West Commerce, and Dolorosa Streets, is a busy shopping and dining area from early morning to late evening, as well as the scene of many San Antonio festivals.

To reach Market Square from the River Walk, follow Commerce Street west across the river to just east of I-10. Or, leave your car and take an inexpensive ride on the VIA streetcars, the open-air trolleys that stop at many downtown San Antonio attractions. (For information on VIA routes, stop by the San Antonio Visitors Center mentioned earlier.)

The history of Market Square goes back to the early 1800s, to a time when Mexico ruled the settlement of San Antonio de Bejar. Fresh produce and meats filled the farmer's market, and pharmaceutical items were available at Botica Guadalupana, today the oldest continually operating pharmacy in town (and a very interesting place to browse, even if you're feeling healthy).

Chili con carne, the state dish of Texas, was invented here in the 1840s. Back then, young girls known as "chili queens" sold the spicy meat and bean concoction from kiosks.

Today Market Square offers a farmer's market, an open-air restaurant and shopping area, and El Mercado, the largest enclosed Mexican-style marketplace in the country. Also located nearby are two historic structures: the Spanish Governor's Palace and Navarro House, home of a Texas patriot.

WHERE TO GO

Farmer's Market. Buy fresh produce here directly from the farmers, starting in the early morning hours. There's a parking deck on the second floor inside the market. Open daily. Free (fee for parking). (210) 299-8600.

El Mercado. Styled after a typical Mexican market, El Mercado's 50 shops sell a rich profusion of goods, from silver jewelry, Mexican dresses, and piñatas to onyx chess sets, leather goods, and much more. Prices are slightly higher than in the Mexican markets, and you can't bargain with the vendors like you can in Mexico. Open daily. Free. (210) 299-8600.

Spanish Governor's Palace. 105 Military Plaza. Part of an old Spanish fort that was built at the site in 1722, this structure was converted to a military commander's residence in 1749. San Antonio was once the capital of the Spanish province of Texas, and the Spanish governors occasionally resided here. The walls are three feet thick, and the home is filled with Spanish colonial antiques. Open daily. Fee. (210) 224-0601.

Jose Navarro Home. 228 S. Laredo St. This was the former residence of a signer of the Texas Declaration of Independence. The adobe and limestone structure includes an office used by Navarro, who was a lawyer and legislator. Open Tuesday through Sunday. Fee. (210) 226-4801.

WHERE TO EAT

Mi Tierra. 218 Produce Row. This is the place to head for an unbeatable Tex-Mex meal that includes homemade tortillas, enchiladas, and *chiliquiles,* a spicy egg and corn tortilla breakfast dish served with refried beans. Open 24 hours for breakfast, lunch, and dinner. $-$$; []. (210) 225-1262.

La Margarita. 102 Produce Row. This establishment also is owned by Mi Tierra and is best known for its excellent fajitas, which are brought to your table in cast-iron skillets. Open for lunch and dinner. $-$$; []. (210) 227-7140.

OUTSIDE DOWNTOWN

Although the downtown area has plenty of attractions, other stops lie on the outskirts of the city, including two large theme parks, a zoo, missions, and botanical gardens.

WHERE TO GO

Sea World of Texas. Ellison Dr. and Westover Hills Blvd., off TX 151; 18 miles northwest of downtown, between Loop 410 and Loop 1604. This 250-acre, $170 million Texas-sized park is the largest marine-life park in the world. It's the home of Shamu the killer whale, plus dolphins, penguins, sea otters, and more. Visitors can enjoy two fast-moving water rides as well as acres of quiet gardens dotted with statues of famous Texans. Entertainment includes 25 shows, featuring a water skiing extravaganza and breathtaking cycling performances.

Other attractions include a beautiful coral reef, a petting pool with people-friendly dolphins, and a Garden of Flags overlooking a map of the United States. Painted on concrete, the map is the size of a parking lot, and children are encouraged to race from "coast to coast." Open daily March through November; weekends only during cooler months. Call for hours. Fee. (800) 422-SWTX.

Fiesta Texas. I-10 and Loop 1604, 15 miles northwest of downtown. This $100 million theme park focuses on the history, culture, and music of San Antonio and the Southwest. Like its sister park, Nashville's Opryland, the main draw of this 200-acre spread is live entertainment. Seven theaters delight visitors with over 60 performances daily, and 13 rides offer fun for all ages. The park has four areas, each featuring a different style of music and entertainment: Hispanic (Los Festivales), German (Spassburg), country-western (Crackaxle Canyon), and rock 'n' roll (Rockville).

Open seasonally March through November; call for hours. Fee. (210) 697-5050.

San Antonio Missions National Historical Park. This national park stretches for nine miles along the San Antonio River and is comprised of four remaining missions (outside of the Alamo) constructed by the Franciscan friars in the 18th century. The missions are active parish churches today and all are open to the public. Each of the four illustrates a different concept of mission life:

Mission San Jose (6539 San Jose Dr.), the most complete structure in the tour, was built in 1720. It has beautiful carvings, 84 rooms that once housed Indians, a restored mill with water wheel, and what may be the only complete mission fort in existence. (210) 229-4770.

Mission Concepción (807 Mission Rd.), built in 1731, holds the title as the oldest unrestored stone church in the country. (210) 229-5732.

Mission San Juan Capistrano (9102 Graff Rd.) was relocated here from East Texas in 1731 but never completed. (210) 229-5734.

Mission San Francisco de la Espada (10040 Espada) was established in 1731. Its original chapel was in ruins by 1778 and the building was reconstructed around 1868. (210) 627-2021.

Open daily. Free.

San Antonio Zoo. 3903 N. St. Mary's St. This world-class zoo features barless "habitat cages" for many of its animals. The cliffs of an abandoned quarry house over 3,000 birds, fish, mammals, and other fauna, making the zoo the third largest animal collection in North America. There's a children's petting area, a reptile house, and an aquarium. Open daily year-round; call for seasonal hours. Fee. (210) 734-7183.

Japanese Tea Gardens. 3800 N. St. Mary's St. by the zoo. San Antonio's semitropical climate encourages the lush flowers, climbing vines, and tall palms found inside this quiet, serene place. The ponds, with beautiful rock bridges and walkways, are home to hundreds of koi, large goldfish. Open daily. Free. (210) 299-3000.

San Antonio Gardens and Halsell Conservatory. 555 Funston Place, near Fort Sam Houston. Roses, herbs, a garden for the blind, and native plants are found within the lovely setting of these 38-acre gardens.

The centerpiece here is the $6.9 million Halsell Conservatory. A futuristic-looking, 90,000-square-foot structure is composed of seven tall glass spires. A self-guided tour of these seven areas takes visitors through the plants and flowers found in different environments, from the desert to the tropics. The conservatory sits partially underground for a cooling effect in the hot Texas summers. Open Tuesday through Sunday. Fee. (210) 821-5115.

Fort Sam Houston Self-Guided Tour. N. New Braunfels Ave. and Stanley Rd. This National Historic Landmark, an army base dating back to 1870, has nine times as many historic buildings as Colonial Williamsburg. These include the residence where General John J. Pershing lived in 1917; the Chinese Camp, once occupied by Chinese who fled Mexico to escape Pancho Villa; and the home where Lieutenant and Mrs. Dwight Eisenhower lived in 1916. Visitors can stroll past the structures (they are not open to the public). Call for hours. Free. (210) 221-6117.

The post also includes two museums. The Fort Sam Houston Museum is filled with exhibits on the site's early days. Open Wednesday through Sunday. Free. (210) 221-1886.

The U.S. Army Medical Department Museum houses exhibits on military medical practices dating back to the Revolutionary War. Open Wednesday through Saturday. Free. (210) 221-6358.

Lone Star Brewery and Buckhorn Hall of Horns. 600 Lone Star Blvd. There's nothing more Texan than Lone Star beer, and you can sample the product at the Buckhorn Saloon. This historic bar once was frequented by short-story writer William Sydney Porter (O. Henry), whose home has been relocated to the brewery grounds.

The Buckhorn Saloon building also contains the Buckhorn Hall of Horns and the Buckhorn Hall of Feathers, each containing their respective mounted specimens of animal horns and Texas birds. Separate buildings house the Hall of Texas History Wax Museum, with figures that recreate Texas's early historic events, and the Buckhorn Hall of Fins, which includes specimens from the Gulf and Texas rivers. Open daily. Fee. (210) 270-9467.

Witte Memorial Museum. 3801 Broadway. This excellent museum focuses on natural history, especially as it relates to the state's Indian, Spanish, and Mexican heritage. Open daily. Fee. (210) 820-2169.

McNay Art Museum. 6000 N. New Braunfels Ave. Located in a Spanish Mediterranean mansion that was once the home of art lover Marion Koogler McNay, the museum houses a nationally known collection of modern art as well as medieval and Gothic works. It also holds the largest collection of European and American graphic art in the Southwest. In the Tobin wing, visitors find one of the country's best theater arts research centers. Open Tuesday through Sunday. Free. (210) 824-5368.

WHERE TO STAY

Sheraton Fiesta. 37 northeast Loop 410. This five-story hotel, built in Spanish colonial style, encircles a beautiful courtyard overhung by arched balconies. An old-fashioned wrought-iron elevator provides direct access from the balconies to the pool area, a nice place to sit and have a drink beneath tall palms. From the hotel's position on the Loop, there's easy access to the theme parks or the zoo. $$-$$$; []. (800) 325-3535 or (210) 366-2424.

ESPECIALLY FOR WINTER TEXANS

Admiralty Park. 1485 N. Ellison Dr., off Loop 1604. This 240-pad RV park is located only minutes from Sea World and Loop 1604. It includes a heated pool, brick patios at each site, free clubhouse movies, cable TV hookups, and organized get-togethers during the winter (potluck dinners, card games, and dominoes). Winter residents can take advantage of special monthly and three-month rates. (800) 999-RVSA.

Day Trip 2

GRUENE
NEW BRAUNFELS

GRUENE

To reach this town pronounced "Green," head south on I-35 for 30 miles to San Marcos (see NORTHEAST FROM SAN ANTONIO, DAY TRIP 2 for attractions in that city.) Continue south for 17 miles to exit 190. Turn west and continue to the intersection with Gruene Road. Turn left on Gruene Road and continue to the community. Although this town is not located on the Texas state map, the exit is identified on interstate signs.

Once a ghost town, Gruene has been transformed into a very popular weekend shopping destination. A historic inn, river rafting, lots of good food, and Texas's oldest dance hall draw visitors from around the state. (See NORTHEAST FROM SAN ANTONIO, DAY TRIP 3.)

NEW BRAUNFELS

Continue south on Gruene Road into neighboring New Braunfels. This city has just about everything to offer travelers, including historic buildings, German food, an enormous water theme park, and enough antique shops to merit the title "The Antique Capital of Texas." Learn more about New Braunfels's numerous attractions in NORTHEAST FROM SAN ANTONIO, DAY TRIP 3.

Day Trip 3

WIMBERLEY
DEVIL'S BACKBONE SCENIC DRIVE
BLANCO

WIMBERLEY

From Austin, follow US 290 west to the small community of Dripping Springs. Turn south on RR 12 and continue 15 miles to Wimberley, a favorite shopping destination from Thursday through Monday. Wimberley's also a great summer destination because of its location on the Blanco River and Cypress Creek. (For the town's attractions, including one of Texas's prettiest swimming holes, see NORTH FROM SAN ANTONIO, DAY TRIP 1.)

DEVIL'S BACKBONE SCENIC DRIVE

From Wimberley, continue south on RR 12 to RR 32. Turn west and sit back for this slow, scenic drive to Fischer, the home of an old-fashioned general store. (Read about these places in NORTH FROM SAN ANTONIO, DAY TRIP 1.)

BLANCO

After passing through Devil's Backbone, continue on RR 32 to US 281. Turn right and head north to Blanco, the home of a beautiful state park and a unique monastery. (See NORTH FROM SAN ANTONIO, DAY TRIP 1.)

To get back home, continue north on US 281. You can turn right on US 290 to go directly to Austin or continue north on US 281 to Johnson City. (For Johnson City attractions, read NORTH FROM SAN ANTONIO, DAY TRIP 2.) At the intersection of TX 71, 18 miles north of Johnson City on US 281, turn east and continue to Austin.

Day Trip 4

COMFORT
SISTERDALE
BOERNE

COMFORT

To reach Comfort, follow US 290 west through Johnson City and Stonewall to US 87. Turn south on US 87 and continue for 23 miles. (As you take this drive, read NORTH FROM SAN ANTONIO, DAY TRIP 2 for attractions along the way.)

Downtown Comfort is a national historic district, filled with the homes and businesses constructed by the town's German pioneers. It's very popular as a weekend antique shopping spot or as a weekday getaway at the historic inn. (For a description of Comfort, see NORTHWEST FROM SAN ANTONIO, DAY TRIP 3.)

SISTERDALE

If you're a wine lover, take a detour on FM 473 to Sisterdale, home of the Sister Creek Winery. See NORTHWEST FROM SAN ANTONIO, DAY TRIP 3 for information on weekday tours.

BOERNE

From Sisterdale, take the 13-mile drive south on FM 1376 to Boerne. If you are traveling directly from Comfort, head south on I-10 for 17 miles. Boerne was also a German community, now home to many antique shops, two caves, and a beautiful park on the Guadalupe River. (Read more about Boerne in NORTH-WEST FROM SAN ANTONIO, DAY TRIP 3.)

From Boerne, you can head back to Austin several ways. For more German atmosphere, drive 42 miles east to New Braunfels on TX 46 (see NORTHEAST

FROM SAN ANTONIO, DAY TRIP 3), then hook into I-35 north to Austin. If you're not in a hurry, head east on TX 46 to US 281, then turn north and take the Devil's Backbone drive. You'll wind up in San Marcos by turning right on FM 306, left on FM 484, then right on FM 32. (See NORTH FROM SAN ANTONIO, DAY TRIP 1 and NORTHEAST FROM SAN ANTONIO, DAY TRIP 2.)

Day Trip 1

JOHNSON CITY
STONEWALL
LUCKENBACH
FREDERICKSBURG
ENCHANTED ROCK STATE PARK

JOHNSON CITY

Head west of Austin on US 290 for 42 miles to the intersection of US 281. Turn north and continue for six miles to LBJ Country. President Johnson's boyhood home is open to visitors, along with the Johnson Settlement where LBJ's grandfather organized cattle drives over a century ago. (Read about these attractions in NORTH FROM SAN ANTONIO, DAY TRIP 2.)

STONEWALL

Continue west on US 290 to Stonewall, the capital of the peach industry and home of the LBJ National and State Historic Parks, where you can tour the LBJ Ranch. This is a great opportunity to visit a working cattle ranch. (For information on these free attractions, see NORTH FROM SAN ANTONIO, DAY TRIP 2.)

LUCKENBACH

To see this tiny community made famous by a country-western song, turn south on FM 1376. Don't rely on signs to this hamlet; they're often stolen by souvenir seekers. (See NORTH FROM SAN ANTONIO, DAY TRIP 2.)

121

FREDERICKSBURG

Retrace your steps from Luckenbach and return to US 290. Continue west to Fredericksburg, a German town that's best known for its shopping and its many historical sites. Weekends are always busy in this charming burg. (See NORTH FROM SAN ANTONIO, DAY TRIP 2.)

ENCHANTED ROCK STATE PARK

If you've saved some energy, head for a look at Enchanted Rock State Park on FM 965. This is the second largest stone formation in the country. (See NORTH FROM SAN ANTONIO, DAY TRIP 2.)

Day Trip 1

MOUNT BONNELL
LAKE TRAVIS
LAKEWAY

This is a popular hot weather day trip. Bring your swimsuit from April through October, along with an old pair of sneakers to navigate the rocky Lake Travis beaches.

MOUNT BONNELL

A beautiful lookout is located within the Austin city limits. Turn left off RR 2222 onto Mount Bonnell Road, which will take you to the highest point in town with a panoramic view of the city and the surrounding hills. Visitors must park and walk up some steep steps to the lookout, but the view is well worth the climb. Free.

WHERE TO EAT

County Line on the Lake. 5204 RR 2222. This is one of the few barbecue restaurants in Texas where you could wear a coat and tie and not look like a "city slicker." Enjoy full table service at this excellent restaurant on Lake Austin, ordering from a menu that features brisket, sausage, and ribs. Open for lunch every day but Saturday; dinner daily. $$-$$$; []. (512) 346-3664.

LAKE TRAVIS

Continue northwest on RR 2222. This winding road is filled with treacherous curves, so take it *slow*. At the intersection of RR 620, you have two choices: turn west onto RR 620 and continue to Mansfield Dam and the remainder of this trip, or turn east to some county parks and Austin's best known outdoor dining spot. This side excursion affords a beautiful drive by some of Austin's most expensive homes.

WHERE TO GO

McGregor/Hippie Hollow Park. From RR 620, turn right onto Comanche Trail. This is a clothing-optional park, the only one in the Austin area. On summer weekends, it is packed with nudists, curious onlookers, and swimmers who want to enjoy a beautiful swimming hole. The parking area is located away from the bathing area. (Nudity is not permitted in the parking lot.)

Onlookers outnumber nudists many weekends, but to see the beach (and the swimmers) you must leave your car and walk down the trail to the water's edge. The swimming area is protected from curious boaters, who are kept at a distance by patrolling Parks Department boats. Fee. Day use only. (512) 266-3314.

Bob Wentz at Windy Point. Comanche Trail, one mile past Hippie Hollow. This park is very popular with windsurfers and scuba divers. Open for camping. Fee. (512) 266-3314.

Slaughter-Leftwich Winery. 107 RR 620. This winery overlooks Lake Travis from an elevation of 3,300 feet above sea level (that's *high* for this state). The elevation helps the vineyards enjoy cool evenings, and, according to the winery, produces a more intense character in their wines. Judge for yourself at tastings held from 1 to 5 p.m. daily. Visitors also can take a free tour on Saturday and Sunday afternoons from September through May, or Thursday through Saturday afternoons during the summer. Free. (512) 266-3331.

WHERE TO EAT

Oasis Cantina Del Lago. 6550 Comanche Trail. Known as "The Sunset Capital of Texas," this restaurant is famous for its open decks overlooking Lake Travis. On weekends this is a popular stop after a day of boating or swimming. The lake views and the surrounding hills provide a lovely backdrop for a sunset meal, the highlight of the day at this unusual restaurant. Open for lunch and dinner daily. $-$$; []. (512) 266-2441.

LAKEWAY

Continue west on RR 620 across Mansfield Dam to the village of Lakeway and Lakeway Resort and Conference Center. This 1,200-person resort community boasts recreational facilities and accommodations for golf and tennis buffs. You can't miss it; just look for the water tower shaped and painted like a golf ball.

Lakeway offers 32 tennis courts, three championship golf courses, a golf academy, a full-service marina, party boats, horseback riding, hayrides, two swimming pools, a fitness center, and a conference center. The World of Tennis, one of the finest tennis facilities in the country, is also located at Lakeway. Guests can stay at the Lakeway Inn, purchasing various packages that include the use of these facilities.

WHAT TO DO

Golf. The Live Oak and the Yaupon 18-hole courses are open to the public. Golf packages in conjunction with the Lakeway Inn also are available. For fees and reservations, call the pro shop at (512) 261-7572 or 261-7573.

Students of the Academy of Golf hone their skills on three full-length holes, a driving range, and a putting green. The Academy is located in The Hills of Lakeway, a private 18-hole course designed by Jack Nicklaus. Reservations required for the Academy. Closed Monday. Call (512) 261-7100.

Tennis. 1 World of Tennis Square. The World of Tennis has 26 world-class indoor courts, including a stadium court. Tennis packages in conjunction with the Lakeway Inn are available. Open daily. Call (512) 261-7222 or 261-7257.

WHERE TO STAY

Lakeway Inn. 101 Lakeway Dr. Adjacent to the marina, this large hotel has 170 rooms featuring Southwest decor and a lake view. Some also have fireplaces and kitchens. A lobby bar serves evening cocktails, and an attractive restaurant offers breakfast, lunch, and dinner. $$$; []. (800) LAKEWAY or (512) 261-6600.

Day Trip 2

MARBLE FALLS
BURNET
BUCHANAN DAM
TOW
KINGSLAND

The Highland Lakes region is comprised of a series of seven lakes that form a back-to-back "stairstep" along the Colorado River. Built in the 1930s by the Lower Colorado River Authority (LCRA) to bring electricity to rural Texas and to control flooding along the Colorado River, the lakes now provide 150 miles of water recreation.

MARBLE FALLS

To reach Marble Falls, take US 183 north of Austin to Cedar Park. (For attractions in this community, see NORTHWEST FROM AUSTIN, DAY TRIP 3.) Turn west on RR 1431 and sit back for a 40-minute ride dotted with cattle ranches, small creeks, and some incredibly beautiful hill country vistas.

Drive south on US 281 to the overlook at the edge of town for a terrific view of the 780-acre Lake Marble Falls. It's said that this sight inspired local songwriter Oscar J. Fox (who also penned "Home on the Range" and "Get Along Little Doggie") to write his popular tune "Hills of Home." Today a marker commemorates this local hero.

While the town may be named for marble, granite is king here. Granite Mountain at the edge of town is the home of a huge quarry that sells pink granite around the country. Visitors are not allowed in the quarry but can observe the operation from the rest stop on the left side of RR 1431.

WHERE TO GO

Lake Marble Falls Cruise. Lakeside Park off US 281 downtown. Take a 90-minute narrated cruise aboard the *General Johnson,* a double-decker, 65-passenger boat. Luncheon cruises sail on Sunday, and gourmet dinner cruises on Thursday, Friday, or Saturday evenings. Open year-round. Fee. (210) 693-6126.

WHERE TO SHOP

Wildlife Sportsman. Located on RR 1431, west of the intersection of US 281. This store stocks plenty of hunting and fishing gadgets and gizmos. It specializes in game calls made to attract everything from deer to wild turkey. The calls are produced in an adjacent building by the Burnham brothers, former owners of this store. Open daily. (210) 693-7072.

BURNET

From Marble Falls, go north to Burnet on US 281, a road lined with fragrant bluebonnet fields in April.

Burnet is the closest town of any size to Lake Buchanan (pronounced "BUCK-an-an"). It's a good place to stop for picnic supplies and sunscreen products during summer visits. (There are few facilities once you leave the city limits.) Outdoor activities are popular throughout the year here, including spelunking and bird-watching.

WHERE TO GO

Fort Croghan Museum. From US 281, turn left onto TX 29 and continue to western edge of town. Fort Croghan was constructed here in the 1840s, one of eight forts built from the Rio Grande to the Trinity Rivers to protect the region from Indian attack. The museum and the adjacent fort sit on the left side of the road. Exhibits include household items used by residents over 100 years ago. You can take a walking tour of the fort, the blacksmith shop, the powder house, and a two-room cabin where one family raised 10 children. Open Thursday through Monday. Free. (512) 756-8281.

Vanishing Texas River Cruise. A few miles past Fort Croghan on TX 29, turn right on FM 2341 and follow signs. This excellent bird-watching cruise is popular with travelers who come to see American bald eagles from November through March. The rest of the year, you might see javelina, wild goats, and white-tail deer. The route takes in 50-foot Fall Creek Falls and a narrow cliff-lined passage on the Colorado River. Cruises also travel past Fall Creek Vineyards on the lake's shore. Open daily. Dinner cruises May through October; reservations required. Open daily. $$; []. Fee. (512) 756-6986.

Inks Lake State Park. From TX 29, turn left onto Park Road 4. This 2,000-acre park offers camping, lakeside picnicking, swimming, and even a golf course. White-tail deer are a common sight during evening hours. Open daily. Fee. For camping reservations, call (512) 793-2223, or write: Rt. 2, P.O. Box 31, Burnet, TX 78611.

Longhorn Cavern State Park. From TX 29, turn left onto Park Road 4. This cavern has few formations but a long and interesting history. In one story, Comanches raided San Antonio, kidnapped a young woman named Mariel King, and brought her back to the cavern, unknowingly followed by three Texas Rangers. A hand-to-hand battle ensued, and Mariel King was rescued. Ending the story with a fairy-tale flourish, Miss King later married one of her rescuers, and the couple lived on in Burnet. The guided tour is nonstrenuous, with wide, well-lit trails through the huge limestone rooms. Open daily. Fee. (512) 756-4680.

From the cavern, return to Burnet by retracing your steps on Park Road 4.

BUCHANAN DAM

Continue driving west on TX 29 to the village of Buchanan Dam, a fishing and retirement community. Lake Buchanan, the jewel of the Highland Lakes, with over 23,000 surface acres of water, is formed by Buchanan Dam, the largest multiarch dam in the world.

Lake Buchanan's own gem is the freshwater pearl. Formed by freshwater mussels in the Colorado River, some pearls found here have been valued at several thousand dollars.

WHERE TO GO

Buchanan Dam Visitors Center. TX 29, at the dam. Here you can find brochures on area campgrounds and activities as well as maps of the Highland Lakes. A museum adjacent to the center provides a look at how the mighty Colorado was tamed. Photographs recount the backbreaking labor involved in the massive project. During spring and summer months, tours of the dam leave on Saturday afternoon; call for times. Open daily. Free. (512) 793-2803.

Buchanan Dam Art Gallery. TX 29, one mile past dam. This is the oldest continually operating artists' cooperative in the country, and it's a great place to buy a bluebonnet painting at a reasonable price. The April arts and crafts show is held here and booths are set up outdoors. During the show local artists sell bluebonnets painted on everything from saw blades to mussel shells. Open daily. Free. (512) 793-2858.

WHERE TO EAT

Big John's Bar-B-Q. TX 29 and RR 1431, two miles west of Buchanan Dam. There's nothing fancy about this old-fashioned barbecue joint, serving sliced beef, ribs, and sausage. Dine indoors or out, on big picnic tables. Open for lunch and dinner, Thursday through Sunday. $$; no []. (512) 793-2261.

TOW

If you're interested in wine, take a drive up to the community of Tow (rhymes with "cow") on the edge of Lake Buchanan. From TX 29, head north eight miles on TX 261, then six miles on FM 2241.

The town's main attraction is the Fall Creek Vineyards, which grow right up to the shores of the lake. You can take a tour of the entire operation and sample the wine made here. Call for weekend tour times. Free. (512) 476-4477.

KINGSLAND

From Tow, you can return to Austin or take a little different route for a peek at another of the Highland Lakes: Lake LBJ. Return to TX 29 by retracing your steps from Tow. Continue west for one mile on TX 29, then turn south on RR 1431 and drive six miles to the retirement and fishing community of Kingsland.

Once named Granite Shoals, Lake LBJ was renamed for President Lyndon Baines Johnson who, as a young senator, brought the lakes project to central Texas. Today the narrow, winding lake is popular with both fishermen and skiers. Edged by steep hills, its clear and calm waters are protected from the winds that often plague the larger lakes.

Kingsland is a sleepy community catering to those who come here to enjoy a few days of bass fishing. Several fishing lodges are located near the junction of the Llano and the Colorado Rivers, where quiet coves afford a catch of black bass, white bass, crappie, catfish, and perch. Be sure to stop at the scenic overlook on RR 1431 just past the edge of town for a grand view of the lake and its shoreline homes.

WHERE TO GO

Kingsland Archaeological Center. East from Kingsland on RR 1431, then right at the Hidden Oaks sign or County Road 126; follow signs to parking area. Discovered in 1988, this archaeological site has yielded nearly 100,000 items dating back to the Paleo-Indian period over 10,000 years ago. Open by appointment. Free. (800) 776-5272, Ext. 3165 or 3227, or (512) 598-5261.

WHERE TO STAY

Longhorn Resort. RR 2900 at Llano River Bridge. This fishing resort has air-conditioned units with kitchenettes, a covered fishing marina, boat stalls, launch ramp, and boats for rent. It also provides camper hookups. $$; []. (915) 388-4343.

Day Trip 3

CEDAR PARK
LEANDER
BERTRAM
BURNET
BUCHANAN DAM
LLANO
MASON

This day trip is filled with winding roads, historic attractions, and natural wonders. It also includes Llano and Mason, two of the best rock-hunting destinations in the country.

Visitors to this hill country must travel over some dirt and gravel roads, especially in rock-hunting areas. Near Mason are numerous low water crossings, and on some back roads you must drive across dry creek beds. Flash flooding is a very real hazard in the hill country, especially during the spring and fall months. Be aware of weather conditions when you make these trips, and never cross swiftly flowing water.

CEDAR PARK

Cedar Park is a 30-minute drive north from Austin via US 183, a congested highway that leads to the Texas hill country.

Now primarily a suburb, there was a time when Cedar Park was called "cedar chopper" country. Cedar choppers were independent men who worked the hilly land to the west, cutting juniper trees to provide fence posts for area ranchers. This generations-old trade is still plied by some hill country families today. The town celebrates its heritage with an annual Cedar Choppers Festival in June.

WHERE TO GO

Austin Steam Train. US 183 and FM 1431. This historic steam train ride is one of the hill country's newest attractions, running from Cedar Park through

Leander and Burnet. Each of the 1930s-era cars is restored to original splendor. The locomotive, donated to the city of Austin by the Southern Pacific Railroad in 1956, resided for many years in a downtown park as playground equipment. After a complete restoration in 1991, she's once again whistling through central Texas. The four-hour ride is offered twice a day on weekends. Fee. (512) 477-8468.

Hill Country Cellars. US 183, north of FM 1431. This winery is noted for a 200-year-old native grapevine transplanted at the site. Acres of vineyards along US 183 produce a Chardonnay, a Hill Country Blush, and a Cabernet Sauvignon. Tours run at 1 p.m. from Tuesday through Thursday, and hourly starting at 1 p.m. on Fridays and weekends. Free. (512) 259-2000.

LEANDER

Continue north on US 183 to neighboring Leander, a small town that boasts many historic markers. To your right as you approach town, you'll see a marker for the Blockhouse Creek subdivision, named for a blockhouse used as an interim prison by the Texas Rangers a century ago.

Another historic marker stands just east of US 183 on FM 2243. The Davis cemetery, as the marker recounts, is the site of a mass grave, a reminder of an Indian attack that ended with the deaths of many pioneers.

WHERE TO SHOP

Lone Star Honey Company. 106 W. Willis. This company sells to retail trade from the Honey Affair store located in front of the processing plant. Here local honey is extracted to produce honey nuts, glazes, and, of course, little honey bears filled with the sticky, sweet product. Closed Sunday and Monday. (512) 259-0524.

BERTRAM

From Leander, continue north on US 183 to the intersection of TX 29. Drive west then on TX 29 for 12 miles to Bertram.

Bertram is a sleepy little town most of the year, but on Labor Day weekend the streets are packed with travelers from around the state who come for the town's annual Oatmeal Festival. They flock to this community for the chance to have oatmeal dropped on their heads from a crop duster, to eat oatmeal cookies, and to watch children dig through wading pools of dried oatmeal for buried pennies. The festival is named for the hamlet of Oatmeal, located six miles south of Bertram on RR 243.

WHERE TO SHOP

Jimmy's Antiques. TX 29. If you're looking for Texas antiques, this is a good place to start. Jimmy's has the usual glassware, china, and jewelry found in most antique stores, but it also handles many local treasures such as Texas Ranger saddlebags, Western saddles, Indian artifacts, and arrowheads. Call for hours. (512) 355-2985.

BURNET

From Bertram, continue west on TX 29 for 10 miles to Burnet, the home of Longhorn Caverns and Fort Croghan. (For information on these and other Burnet attractions, see NORTHWEST FROM AUSTIN, DAY TRIP 2.)

BUCHANAN DAM

Buchanan Dam, located on the shores of Lake Buchanan, is a resort and retirement community located 13 miles west of Burnet on TX 29.

Rock hunters are interested in Lake Buchanan's freshwater pearls. Formed by mussels in the Colorado River, some pearls have been valued at several thousand dollars. For information on Buchanan Dam, see NORTHWEST FROM AUSTIN, DAY TRIP 2.

LLANO

Continuing west on TX 29 from Buchanan Dam, you'll see more and more granite outcroppings, huge boulders protruding from the rugged land. This entire region is called the Llano Uplift, a geological formation caused by igneous rocks from 40 miles below ground being pushed up to the surface.

As a result of the formation, the rich minerals found here turned Llano into a boomtown in the 1880s. The place is still a collector's paradise, with over 240 different rocks and minerals discovered in the region. The area's granite, feldspar, graphite, and talc have commercial value, while the more precious yields, such as garnet, amethyst, tourmaline, quartz—even gold and silver—are sought by eager visiting rock hounds.

Public rock hunting is allowed on the Llano River in town. From the courthouse square, head east on Sandstone Street to Ash Street and turn left. There is a small dirt parking area to your left. Unless you're in a four-wheel drive, park here and walk down the steep dirt road. The riverbanks are dotted with rocks of all varieties and offer some pretty picnic spots as well. To have a look at Llano's rocks and minerals before you begin your search (or to buy some if your hunt was unsuccessful), stop by the Llano Uplift Rock Shop downtown and talk to owner Billy Hazlewood.

If you're interested in more extensive rock hunting, the Llano County Chamber of Commerce at 700 Bessemer Avenue (TX 16) or (915) 247-5354 can provide a list of private landowners who allow collectors on their land.

WHERE TO GO

Llano County Historical Museum. 310 Bessemer Ave. (TX 16). Visitors find this museum housed in the old Bruhl Drugstore, with displays on the area's early Indian history and Llano's boomtown days. An exhibit contains samples of Llano's many rocks and minerals. Open Tuesday through Sunday during the summer, Friday through Sunday after Labor Day. Free. (915) 247-4598.

Walking Tour of Llano. Stop by the Chamber of Commerce office (700 Bessemer Ave.) Monday through Friday for a brochure outlining 26 historic stops in town. Free. (915) 247-5354.

WHERE TO SHOP

Llano Uplift Rock Shop. 805 Berry St., on the square. This is a store for serious rock hounds and for curious travelers who'd like to take home a sample of Llano's offerings without spending a day in the field. Here numerous rocks and minerals are sold, as well as jewelry, gold panning equipment, and lapidary supplies. Open Wednesday through Sunday. (915) 247-3747.

WHERE TO STAY

The Badu House. 601 Bessemer Ave. (TX 16). This two-story stone and brick inn, circa 1891, was the former home of mineralogist N. J. Badu, who put Llano on the map by discovering the mineral llanite here at the turn of the century. The building has been elegantly renovated, and all eight bedrooms feature private baths, ceiling fans, air-conditioning, and period furnishings. Late afternoon cocktails are served in a club adjacent to the restaurant offering everything from filet mignon to oven-roasted quail. $$-$$$; []. (915) 247-4304.

Dabbs Hotel. 112 E. Burnet St., behind Llano Museum. At the turn of the century, this railroad hotel was the last outpost of civilization before heading west. Today's guests are treated to 12 quiet rooms with period furnishings, double beds, a breezy screened porch, and peaceful atmosphere overlooking the Llano River. Saturday nights feature Western cookouts. Dinner reservations required. $; no []. (915) 247-7905.

WHERE TO EAT

Inman's Kitchen and Catering Service. 809 W. Young (TX 29 west). Barbecue is king here, including beef brisket, chicken, pork, and the restaurant's specialty: turkey sausage. This spot is more elegant than many barbecue restaurants, with a carpeted, air-conditioned dining area. Lunch and dinner served

Monday through Saturday; open Sundays during deer season. $; no []. (915) 247-5257.

MASON

From Llano, continue west on TX 29 for 34 miles to Mason, once the home of the late Fred Gipson, author of *Old Yeller*. Like neighboring Llano, the land around Mason is rocky and dotted with granite.

Mason was settled by cattle ranchers and German families who came from nearby Fredericksburg. In 1851, Fort Mason was built on a hilltop to afford a better look at oncoming Comanches. (Fort Mason's best known soldier was Lieutenant Colonel Robert E. Lee.) Constructed of sandstone, in 1869 the fort was dismantled and the sandstone rocks were used to build local businesses and homes.

Rock hounds come to Mason County today in search of topaz, the Texas state gem, which develops in colors ranging from clear to sky blue. Most local topaz turns up near the small communities of Streeter, Grit, and Katemcy, all north and northeast of Mason. Searchers usually find the stones in streambeds and ravines by using picks and shovels to loosen rocks and a wire screen to sift.

WHERE TO GO

Fort Mason. Follow Post Hill St. south from courthouse to Post Hill. These reconstructed officers' quarters are furnished with typical 1850s belongings as well as photographs from Mason's early days. The back porch has an unbeatable view of the town below and miles of hill country beyond. Open daily. Free.

Mason National Bank Slide Show. 103 Westmoreland, on the square. A 15-minute slide show about the area's attractions and history is offered here during banking hours. Open Monday through Friday. Free. (915) 347-5911.

Gene Zesch Wood Carving Display at The Commercial Bank. 100 Moody St., on the square. Gene Zesch is one of Mason's most famous citizens, known for his humorous woodcarvings of modern cowboys. His work was collected by President Johnson and is sold in galleries nationally. This exhibit features woodcarvings and bronzes made by the artist. Open Monday through Friday. Free. (915) 347-6324.

Mason County Museum. 300 Moody St., south of the square. This local history museum is housed in an old elementary school, built in 1887. The contents include typical items used by area ranchers and housewives a century ago, from toys to needlework to farm equipment. There is also a display of local rocks and minerals. Open weekdays. Free. (915) 347-6411 or 347-5752.

Seaquist House. 400 Broad St. This sandstone mansion, with 22 rooms and 15 fireplaces, was built in the 1880s for a local banker. Today visitors can tour the third floor ballroom, billiards room, and formal parlor and dining room. Tours run by appointment only. Fee. (915) 347-6659 or 347-5413.

Eckert James River Bat Cave. Write or call the Mason Chamber of Commerce (P.O. Box 156, Mason, TX 76856; 915-347-5758) for directions and a map to this bat cave, located about 13 miles south of Mason. The cavern is home to about six million Mexican free-tail bats. This is a "maternity cave," used during the spring and summer months by female bats to bear and rear their young. You can view the evening flight out of the cave, a sight heralded by high-pitched sounds. Open daily. Free.

White-tail Deer Hunting. Mason County claims to have more white-tail deer per acre than any other county in Texas. Hunters flock here from around the Southwest to stalk deer during the winter months. For information on hunting licenses, call the Mason Chamber of Commerce (915-347-5758) well before deer season begins.

Topaz Hunting. Two private areas charge a daily fee of $10 per person for topaz hunting. Visitors must bring their own equipment (including water during warm summer months) and may keep whatever they find. The following ranches offer topaz hunting from mid-January through October:

Wayne Hofmann Ranch, c/o Wesley Loeffler, Menard Rt., Mason, TX 76856; (915) 347-6415.

Garner Seaquist Ranch, P.O. Box 35, Mason, TX 76856; (915) 347-5413. (This ranch also offers camping facilities, both tent sites and camper hookups with water, electricity, and showers.)

WHERE TO SHOP

Country Collectibles. US 87 north. If your search for topaz comes up empty, stop by this antique store, which sells topaz and other stones indigenous to the area plus arrowheads, willow furniture, and collectibles of every description. (915) 347-5249.

WHERE TO STAY

Mason County is filled with bed and breakfast accommodations, RV campsites, and guest ranches located outside of town. For a free copy of their "Bed and Breakfast and RV Sites" brochure, contact the Mason Chamber of Commerce at (915) 347-5758, or write: P.O. Box 156, Mason, TX 76856.

Regional Information

SAN ANTONIO

NORTH FROM SAN ANTONIO

Day Trip 1

Blanco Chamber of Commerce
P.O. Box 626
Blanco, TX 78606
(210) 833-5101

Wimberley Chamber of Commerce
P.O. Box 12
Wimberley, TX 78676
(512) 847-2201

Day Trip 2

Johnson City Chamber of Commerce
P.O. Box 485
Johnson City, TX 78636
(210) 868-7684

Fredericksburg Convention and Visitors Bureau
P.O. Box 506
Fredericksburg, TX 78624
(210) 997-6523

NORTHEAST FROM SAN ANTONIO

Day Trip 1

Austin Convention and Visitors Bureau
P.O. Box 2990
Austin, TX 78769
(800) 926-2282 or (512) 474-5171

Day Trip 2

San Marcos Chamber of Commerce
P.O. Box 2310
San Marcos, TX 78667
(800) 782-7653

Buda City Hall
P.O. Box 1218
Buda, TX 78610
(512) 295-6331

Day Trip 3

New Braunfels Chamber of Commerce
390 S. Seguin St.
New Braunfels, TX 78130
(800) 572-2626

EAST FROM SAN ANTONIO

Day Trip 1

Luling Area Chamber of Commerce
P.O. Box 710
Luling, TX 78648
(210) 875-3214

Flatonia Chamber of Commerce
P.O. Box 651
Flatonia, TX 78941
(512) 865-3920

Schulenburg Chamber of Commerce
P.O. Box 65
Schulenburg, TX 78956
(409) 743-4514

Day Trip 2

Seguin-Guadalupe County Chamber of Commerce
P.O. Box 710
Seguin, TX 78156
(210) 379-6382

Gonzales Chamber of Commerce
P.O. Box 134
Gonzales, TX 78629
(210) 672-6532

Shiner Chamber of Commerce
810 N. Avenue E
P.O. Box 221
Shiner, TX 77984
(512) 594-4180

Yoakum Chamber of Commerce
P.O. Box 591
Yoakum, TX 77995
(512) 293-2309

SOUTHEAST FROM SAN ANTONIO

Day Trip 1

Goliad Chamber of Commerce
P.O. Box 606
Goliad, TX 77963
(512) 645-3563

SOUTH FROM SAN ANTONIO

Day Trip 1

Aransas Pass Chamber of Commerce
452 Cleveland Blvd.
Aransas Pass, TX 78336
(512) 758-3713

Port Aransas Chamber of Commerce
P.O. Box 356
Port Aransas, TX 78373
(800) 242-3084 or (800) 45-COAST

Rockport-Fulton Area Chamber of Commerce
P.O. Box 1055
Rockport, TX 78382
(800) 242-0071 or (800) 826-6441

Day Trip 2

Corpus Christi Convention and Visitors Bureau
P.O. Box 2664
Corpus Christi, TX 78403
(800) 766-BEACH

SOUTHWEST FROM SAN ANTONIO

Day Trip 1

Laredo Area Chamber of Commerce
P.O. Box 790
Laredo, TX 78042
(210) 722-9895

WEST FROM SAN ANTONIO

Day Trip 1

Eagle Pass Chamber of Commerce
P.O. Box 1188
Eagle Pass, TX 78852
(210) 773-3224

Day Trip 2

Castroville Chamber of Commerce
P.O. Box 572
Castroville, TX 78009
(210) 538-3142

Uvalde Chamber of Commerce
P.O. Box 706
Uvalde, TX 78802
(210) 278-3361

Day Trip 3

Del Rio Area Chamber of Commerce
1915 Avenue F
Del Rio, TX 78840
(210) 775-3551

NORTHWEST FROM SAN ANTONIO

Day Trip 1

Bandera County Chamber of Commerce
P.O. Box 171
Bandera, TX 78003
(800) 364-3833

Day Trip 2

Kerrville Convention and Visitors Bureau
1200 Sidney Baker
Kerrville, TX 78028
(800) 221-7958 in Texas; (210) 896-1155

West Kerr County Chamber of Commerce
P.O. Box 1006
Ingram, TX 78025
(210) 367-4322

Day Trip 3

Greater Boerne Area Chamber of Commerce
One Main Plaza
P.O. Box 1888
Boerne, TX 78006
(210) 249-8000

Comfort Chamber of Commerce
P.O. Box 777
Comfort, TX 78013
(210) 995-3131

AUSTIN

NORTH FROM AUSTIN

Day Trip 1

Round Rock Chamber of Commerce
212 E. Main St.
Round Rock, TX 78664
(800) 747-3479 or (512) 255-5805

Georgetown Convention and Visitors Bureau
P.O. Box 409
Georgetown, TX 78627
(512) 869-3545

Salado Chamber of Commerce
P.O. Box 81
Salado, TX 76571
(817) 947-5040

Belton Area Chamber of Commerce
P.O. Box 659
Belton, TX 76513
(817) 939-3551

Temple Chamber of Commerce
P.O. Box 158
Temple, TX 76503
(817) 773-2105

Day Trip 2

Waco Tourist Information Center
P.O. Box 2570
Waco, TX 76702
(800) WACO-FUN

NORTHEAST FROM AUSTIN

Day Trip 1

Taylor Chamber of Commerce
P.O. Box 231
Taylor, TX 76574
(512) 352-6364

Calvert Chamber of Commerce
P.O. Box 506
Calvert, TX 77837
(409) 364-2559

EAST FROM AUSTIN

Day Trip 1

Burton Chamber of Commerce
P.O. Box 132
Burton, TX 77835
(409) 289-2321

Brenham-Washington County Convention and Visitors Bureau
314 S. Austin
Brenham, TX 77833
(409) 836-3695

SOUTHEAST FROM AUSTIN

Day Trip 1

Bastrop Chamber of Commerce
P.O. Box 681
Bastrop, TX 78602
(512) 321-2419

Smithville Chamber of Commerce
P.O. Box 716
Smithville, TX 78957
(512) 237-2313

LaGrange Chamber of Commerce
129 N. Main St.
La Grange, TX 78945
(409) 968-5756

SOUTH FROM AUSTIN

Day Trip 1

Lockhart Chamber of Commerce
P.O. Box 840
Lockhart, TX 78644
(512) 398-2818

See also EAST FROM SAN ANTONIO, Day Trips 1 and 2

Day Trip 2

See NORTHEAST FROM SAN ANTONIO, Day Trip 2

SOUTHWEST FROM AUSTIN

Day Trip 1

San Antonio Convention and Visitors Bureau
P.O. Box 2277
San Antonio, TX 78298
(800) 447-3372 or (210) 270-8700

Day Trip 2

See NORTHEAST FROM SAN ANTONIO, Day Trip 3

Day Trip 3

See NORTH FROM SAN ANTONIO, Day Trip 1

Day Trip 4

See NORTHWEST FROM SAN ANTONIO, Day Trip 3

WEST FROM AUSTIN

Day Trip 1

See NORTH FROM SAN ANTONIO, Day Trip 2

NORTHWEST FROM AUSTIN

Day Trip 1

Lakeway
One World of Tennis Square
Austin, TX 78738
(512) 261-6000

Day Trip 2

Highland Lakes Tourist Association
P.O. Box 294
Buchanan Dam, TX 78609
(512) 793-6666

Marble Falls Chamber of Commerce
801 US 281
Marble Falls, TX 78654
(210) 693-4449

Burnet Chamber of Commerce
Drawer M
Burnet, TX 78611
(512) 756-4297

Lake Buchanan Chamber of Commerce
P.O. Box 294
Buchanan Dam, TX 78609
(512) 793-2803

Kingsland Chamber of Commerce
P.O. Box 465
Kingsland, TX 78639
(915) 388-6211

Day Trip 3

Cedar Park Chamber of Commerce
200 S. Bell Blvd.
P.O. Box 1464
Cedar Park, TX 78613
(512) 258-8007

Leander Chamber of Commerce
200 W. Willis
P.O. Box 556
Leander, TX 78641
(512) 259-1907

Llano Chamber of Commerce
700 Bessemer Ave.
Llano, TX 78643
(915) 247-5354

Mason Chamber of Commerce
P.O. Box 156
Mason, TX 76856
(915) 347-5758

Festivals and Celebrations

Texas undoubtedly has more festivals than any other state. Regardless of the weekend, you'll find some town whooping it up with parades, music, and lots of food. There are festivals for every interest, whether yours is pioneer heritage, German food, or watermelons.

For a quarterly list of Texas's annual events, write the Texas Department of Highways and Public Transportation for their free Texas events calendar at P.O. Box 5064, Austin, TX 78763, or call (800) 8888-TEX or (800) 452-9292.

You can also receive a free annual events calendar from the Texas Festivals Association at 900 Congress, Suite 301, Austin, TX 78701; (512) 476-4472.

JANUARY

World Mohair Extravaganza, Kerrville. This two-day festival celebrates the mohair industry with goat shearing, spinning demonstrations, and even a fashion show featuring mohair clothing. (800) 221-7958 or (210) 866-3424.

FEBRUARY

George Washington's Birthday Celebration, Laredo and Nuevo Laredo. The border towns of Laredo and Nuevo Laredo celebrate from Tuesday through Saturday with a charro rodeo, games, and a general party atmosphere. (210) 722-9895.

Texas Independence Celebration, Washington-on-the-Brazos. Held at the end of February and beginning of March, this celebration of the signing of the Texas Declaration of Independence in 1836 includes demonstrations of pioneer cooking, frontier crafts, and folk music. There's even a reenactment of the signing. (409) 878-2461 or 836-3695.

Land of Leather Days, Yoakum. The last weekend in February celebrates the importance of leather in "The Leather Capital of the World." There are saddle-making demonstrations, plus a chili cookoff, and plenty of leather products for sale. (512) 293-2309.

Winterfest, Corpus Christi. This festival salutes the many winter Texans in the area with a Parade of Flags, an arts and crafts show, dances, and entertainment. (800) 678-OCEAN.

MARCH

Fulton Oysterfest, Fulton. Spend the first weekend in March downing fried or raw oysters to celebrate the culmination of the oyster harvest. Besides oyster

145

eating and shucking contests, there are games, entertainment, and dances. (800) 24-0071 or (512) 729-7529.

National Rattlesnake Sacking Championship and Roundup, Taylor. This is one of the most unusual annual events in Texas, held on the first weekend of the month. Two-man teams compete in this national event to see who can sack 10 rattlers in the shortest amount of time. (512) 352-6364.

APRIL

Highland Lakes Bluebonnet Trail, Burnet, Buchanan Dam, Llano, and area communities. The fragrant bluebonnet is the state flower of Texas. For two weekends in early April, a self-guided driving tour will take you past the area's prettiest bluebonnet fields. Each town on the trail, from Burnet to Llano, celebrates with art shows, races, and a festival atmosphere. (512) 793-6666.

Bluebonnet Festival, Schulenburg. On the second Saturday in April, tour fields of fragrant bluebonnets and visit the area's painted churches. (409) 743-4514.

Buccaneer Days, Corpus Christi. Near the end of April Corpus Christi's swashbuckling days are relived with pioneer parades, a terrific fireworks display over the bay, and a huge carnival. (800) 678-OCEAN or (512) 882-3242.

Easter Fires, Fredericksburg. Relive the Easter fires of 1847, when Comanches sat in the hills over Fredericksburg while women and children awaited the results of a peace talk. Mothers calmed their children's fears by explaining that the campfires belonged to the Easter bunny. This story is recreated in a pageant on the Saturday eve before Easter. Advance tickets are suggested. Fredericksburg Easter Fires, P.O. Box 506, Fredericksburg, TX 78624, or (210) 997-6523.

Fiesta, San Antonio. The granddaddy of San Antonio's festivals, this week-long celebration includes a water parade, a battle of flowers, art shows, lots of great food, and more. Find out about parking alternatives before heading into the congested River Walk area where the festival takes place. (800) 447-3372 or (210) 270-8700.

MAY

Chisholm Trail Roundup, Lockhart. Relive the Battle of Plum Creek, where the Texas militia joined forces with Tonkowa Indians to defeat a band of Comanches. You can also enjoy a dance, a parade, and a carnival. (512) 398-2818.

Cinco de Mayo and State Menudo Cookoff, San Marcos. This festival is held on the weekend closest to Cinco de Mayo, or May Fifth, the celebration of the Mexican victory over the French. Besides a carnival and musical performances, there's plenty of Mexican food, including *menudo* (a dish made from tripe, hominy, and spices). (800) 782-7653.

Funteer Days, Bandera. If they had festivals back in the Wild West days, they must have looked like this one. Tobacco spitting contests, country-western dances, fiddlin' contests, and an Old West parade draw crowds for this weekend late in May. (800) 364-3833.

Kerrville Folk Festival, Kerrville. This is one of the biggest outdoor music festivals in the state. For 11 days, the banks of the Guadalupe River are lined with music lovers who come to hear both local and nationally known performers. (800) 221-7958 in Texas or (210) 227-3600.

Fiesta Laguna Gloria, Austin. This festival combines art with the spirit of a Mexican party, complete with mariachis and Mexican folk dancers. Over 200 artists and craftsmen bring their work to this mid-May celebration. (800) 926-2282 or (512) 474-5171.

JUNE

Indian Hobbyists Meeting, Llano. Over 300 people come here in mid-June from around the state, setting up tepees and keeping alive Indian traditions. There's trading of Indian artifacts and products and a relaxed atmosphere. (915) 247-5354.

Cedar Chopper Festival, Cedar Park. This festival, always held the second Saturday of June, celebrates the "cedar chopper" heritage of the area. At one time, people here made their living cutting juniper trees into fence posts. Starting with a parade, the festival includes arts and crafts, rides, and a dance. (512) 258-8007.

Peach Jamboree, Stonewall. The peach capital of Texas shows off its crop on the third Friday and Saturday of June. The local peach pit spitting record is over 28 feet. (210) 644-2413.

Watermelon Thump, Luling. On the last Thursday, Friday, and Saturday of June, you can enjoy seed-spitting contests, watermelon-eating contests, and a champion melon judging. There's also an arts and crafts show, carnivals, live entertainment, and street dances. A Guinness World Record was set here in 1989 for spitting a watermelon seed almost 69 feet. (210) 875-3214.

JULY

Half Moon Holidays Shiner. On the first Sunday in July, Shiner celebrates summer with a chili cookoff, barbecue dinner, carnival, horseshoe-pitching tournament, dance, and lots of music. (512) 594-4180.

Sam Bass Days, Round Rock. Come to Round Rock on the Friday and Saturday after Fourth of July to watch a reenactment of the infamous shoot-out between outlaw Sam Bass and the Texas Rangers. There's also plenty of food, games, and the atmosphere of a summer festival. (800) 747-3479.

Deep Sea Roundup, Port Aransas. Fishermen come from everywhere for a chance at the purse in the biggest fishing tournament on this part of the coast, held the weekend after July fourth. Stay at the pier and watch the competitors weigh in their catch. (800) 242-3084.

International Apple Festival, Medina. This celebration of the apple harvest is held in late July, with lots of apple pies, barbecue, and games. (210) 589-2588.

AUGUST

Texas Folklife Festival, San Antonio. Texas's many cultures are represented in this four-day event in early August. Costumed craftsmen demonstrate how to make a horse-hair rope, pluck a goose, or shuck corn. Folk dancers perform everything from the polka to Indian dances. Plenty of traditional and ethnic cuisine is served. This festival is held at the Institute of Texan Cultures at HemisFair Park. (800) 447-3372 or (210) 226-7651.

AquaFest, Austin. The Southwest's largest music festival stretches over three consecutive weekends, with multiple stages featuring from rock to country-western to zydeco. Several big names always perform, along with lots of local talent. There are also jet ski demonstrations, yacht races, a lighted water parade, and a midway for the kids. (800) 926-2282 or (512) 472-5664.

International Barbecue Cookoff, Taylor. Barbecue beef, chicken, and sausage reign supreme at most Texas barbecue joints, but this mid-August cook-off also features seafood, lamb, goat, and even wild game. Over 100 teams compete in categories ranging from showmanship to most elaborate cooking equipment. (512) 352-6364.

SEPTEMBER

Oatmeal Festival, Bertram. Where else can you have dry oatmeal poured over your head from a low-flying crop duster? This Labor Day weekend festival is named for the nearby community of Oatmeal, and all the events from the street parade to the midway continue the theme. (512) 355-2197 or 355-2268.

Port A Days, Port Aransas. This three-day farewell-to-summer festival starts with an "anything that will float but a boat" parade, and includes a gumbo cookoff, a street dance, a horseshoe tournament, and lots of fine Gulf food. (800) 242-3084 or 221-9198.

Hummer/Bird Celebration, Rockport. Thousands of migrating humming-birds stop to refuel in Rockport, which celebrates the event with four days of lectures by birding authorities, arts and crafts displays, boat tours, and Audubon guided bus tours to sites swarming with as many as 150 hummingbirds. (800) 242-0071 or 826-6441.

Deis y Seis de Septiembre, Del Rio. First named San Felipe, Del Rio celebrates its historic past with Mexican food, Mexican bingo, and plenty of music. (210) 775-3551.

OCTOBER

Oktoberfest, Fredericksburg. On the first weekend in October, you can head to the "Old Country" by driving to this German hill country town. You'll find polka dancing and sausage galore, as well as arts and crafts, a street dance, and rides for the kids. Friday through Sunday. (210) 997-6523.

"Come and Take It" Days, Gonzales. This reenactment of the famous "Come and Take It" skirmish that started the Texas Revolution takes place the weekend closest to October 2. Over 30,000 visitors come to enjoy the battle as well as the games, a carnival, a biergarten, helicopter rides, and a street dance. (210) 672-6532.

Oktoberfest, Round Top. Unlike other Oktoberfest celebrations, this one does it in the pioneer spirit, with demonstrations on everything from soap making to spinning. (409) 278-3530.

Llano Heritage Days, Llano. During mid-October this hill country town remembers its historic roots with Wild West shoot-outs, living history exhibits, wagon rides, and antique shows. (915) 247-5354.

Old Leander Days, Leander. This fall festival includes a parade, a carnival, a domino tournament, and a country-western dance. (512) 259-1907.

Fiesta de Amistad, Del Rio and Ciudad Acuña. The friendship between Del Rio and Ciudad Acuña is celebrated with a chili cookoff, a battle of the bands, and an international parade—the only one that starts in one country and ends in another. (210) 775-3551.

Harvest Moon Festival, Calvert. Shop for antiques, watch Civil War re-enactments or a Wild West shoot-out, or take a ride on a hot air balloon in this mid-October celebration of autumn. (409) 364-2909 or 364-2774.

Chilispiel, Flatonia. When tiny Flatonia needed a doctor years ago, local citizens decided to send a hometown girl to medical school. To fund her education, they began this chili cookoff (now the second largest in Texas) and festival held in late October. There's lots of music, a quilt show, "the world's largest tented biergarten," and a barbecue cookoff as well. (512) 865-3920.

NOVEMBER

Wurstfest, New Braunfels. Early in November, pull on your lederhosen, take out your beer stein, and join the fun at this celebration of sausage making. One of the largest German festivals in the country, Wurstfest features oompah bands and great German food. (800) 221-4369 or (210) 625-2385.

Fall Arts Trail, Buchanan Dam, Kingsland, Burnet, Llano, and Marble Falls. The Highland Lakes Arts Council sponsors this early November festival along the same route as the spring Bluebonnet Festival. Each community has an art show, from the Highland Lakes Porcelain Art Club show in Kingsland to Buchanan Dam's Arts and Crafts Gallery, the oldest artists' cooperative in the United States. (512) 793-6666.

Gathering of the Scottish Clans, Salado. Get out your kilt for this unusual early November festival that draws Scottish descendants from around the state. If you have Scottish ancestry, you can learn more about your family genealogy. Even if you're not a lass or laddie, enjoy traditional folk dances, Highland games, lots of bagpipe music, and Scottish foods like meat pies and scones. (817) 947-5232 or 947-5040.

Winter Texan Friendship Rally, Temple. This four-day event is held at the Outdoor America Mall and is aimed at RVers. It includes vendor exhibits, catered meals, and entertainment. (817) 771-5466.

DECEMBER

Fort Croghan Spirit of Christmas Past, Burnet. Held in early December, this festival is a recreation of a pioneer Christmas. A holiday dinner is served in the Old Country Store, then the festivities move to Fort Croghan, lit by glowing lanterns. Visitors on the candlelight tour are met by carolers and costumed docents. (512) 756-4297.

Harbor Lights, Corpus Christi. The Christmas spirit starts in Corpus Christi with the Christmas Tree Forest at the Art Museum of South Texas, with all trees decorated on a special theme. Santa Claus arrives in the port city aboard, what else, a boat, and the bayfront is lit with thousands of tiny lights. (800) 678-OCEAN.

Christmas Lighting Tour, Johnson City, Llano Fredericksburg, Blanco, and Marble Falls. The hill country joins together for this trail of Christmas lights and festivities. Blanco's historic courthouse square is lit with festive lights, and Marble Falls celebrates "Christmas by the Lake" with shopping and food. Fredericksburg puts on a Kinderfest, Kristkindl Market, and candlelight tours of homes. Llano features a Santa Land. Johnson City, the boyhood home of LBJ, is aglow with over a quarter million lights.

On the first weekend, there's a special Pick-Up Truck Parade (only in Texas!), with decorated trucks to ring in the Christmas season. Finally, Stonewall celebrates with an annual tree lighting at the LBJ Park, a live nativity scene, and pioneer foods served by candlelight at the Sauer-Beckman Farm. (210) 868-7684 or 644-2252.

Appendix A.
Shopping in Mexico

No trip to the Mexican border is complete without some shopping. For many South Texans, this is a chance to purchase quality jewelry, blankets, and liquor at prices far below those in the United States.

All shopping in the border towns is done with American currency. The "Casa de Cambio" signs are seen on many streets, but you do not need to exchange currency before you go. Most shopkeepers speak fluent English, especially in Nuevo Laredo and Ciudad Acuña. In Piedras Negras, bring along a Spanish-English dictionary if you plan to venture beyond the market area.

Buying is usually done by *negociación*. Many stores do not label items with a price. The shopkeeper names a price, one higher than he knows is acceptable. The shopper asks for the "best price," and a friendly haggling ensues. Usually both the merchant and the shopper part company happy with their deal.

Making purchases from street vendors is also done through *negociación*. Street vendors have good prices on paper flowers, hammocks, lace tablecloths, inlaid earrings (not sterling silver), and wood carvings.

Currently silver jewelry is the hottest item in border shops. Look for the "921" stamp on the back of the piece to ensure silver quality. Many of the better stores sell jewelry by weight, with a fixed price per ounce. Even so, silver is very reasonably priced in comparison to U.S. stores. Silver and black onyx jewelry also represents a good bargain.

Glass, especially pitchers, bowls, and blue-rimmed drinking glasses, and leather goods also make excellent purchases. Onyx chess sets, papier-mâché fruits and vegetables, elaborately embroidered Mexican dresses, and woven blankets are other good buys.

Heading home, you must cross through U.S. customs, located on the American side of the International Bridge.

Certain items cannot be carried back into the United States. These include fruits, vegetables, animals and birds, and meats (including canned items). Fireworks, switchblade knives (sold by nearly every street vendor), firearms, liquor-filled candy, lottery tickets, and items made from endangered species will be confiscated. Although you can go to the *pharmacia* and buy any item without a prescription, you cannot bring it back to the United States. This includes Mexican diet pills.

Be careful of counterfeit trademark items, such as $40 Rolex watches sold in many shops. These can be seized, and you must forfeit them if stopped by a customs official.

When you return to the United States, the customs official will ask if you are an American citizen. He may ask what you purchased, and he may also ask to see your purchases and other belongings.

You must also pass by a booth to pay tax on imported liquor and cigarettes. If you are over 21 years of age, you may bring back one liter of liquor and 200 cigarettes. Texas places a tax on both these items, but the savings is still substantial, especially on items like Mexican beer and tequila.

As far as other goods, you may return with $400 worth of merchandise without paying duty. Every person in your party, regardless of age, has this $400 exemption.

If you've made large purchases, save your receipts. You must pay a 10% duty on goods over $400 but less than $1,400.

For more information on customs, obtain Publication 512, "Know Before You Go" by writing: U.S. Customs Service, P.O. Box 7407, Washington, DC 20044.

Appendix B. Entering Mexico

A trip across the border is easy, safe, and fun. The easiest way to enter Mexico is by walking across the International Bridge or *Puente Internacional* for a small toll. On return, pay another small toll, walk across the bridge, then head through U.S. customs. (See the previous appendix, "Shopping in Mexico," for details.)

Every border town has taxi service into and out of Mexico. The ride is only a few dollars each way. Call the local chamber of commerce for information on transportation to Mexican shopping areas or dining spots.

Driving into Mexico can be a somewhat frightening prospect because auto mishaps are a criminal rather than civil offense across the border. If you are in a wreck, you might find yourself in a Mexican jail, a sure way to spoil a vacation.

If you are a confident driver, then by all means drive into Mexico. Short-term Mexican insurance is required of every driver. Unless you live near the border and carry a special rider on your policy, your car insurance is probably not valid in Mexico. Every Texas border town has several insurance companies that sell short-term Mexican insurance. Call the local chamber of commerce for information on these companies.

Once you are in Mexico, look for secured parking. The larger restaurants have pay parking lots, and these are preferable to parking on the streets.

Remember that Mexican speed signs are posted in kilometers. Also, Mexican traffic lights are slightly different than our own. When you see a yellow light begin to blink, it means that yellow will soon change to red.

Mexican streets are very narrow, and often one way, especially in the main tourist areas. One-way streets are common.

Appendix C.
Especially for Winter Texans

If you're among the many lucky travelers who've adopted the Lone Star state as their winter home, welcome to Texas. You've chosen a destination where you can enjoy the excitement of the West, the zest of Old Mexico, the tranquility of the Gulf, and the history of a rambunctious republic, all in one journey. Some of the best seasons and reasons to see the state include the changing post oak leaves in fall, the glittering Christmas festivals, and the often sunny Texas winter days.

To introduce you to winter attractions throughout the state, there's a free publication available called *Winter Texan Magazine*. It includes information on campgrounds, motel discounts for winter Texans, festivals, and attractions. Call the magazine at (800) 728-1287 or the State Department of Highways and Public Transportation at (800) 8888-TEX or (800) 452-9292.

Texas has an excellent network of state parks, most which provide campsites with hookups. Generally there is a 14-consecutive-days limit for camping at each park.

Winter Texans will be interested in the two different discount programs available at state parks. If you are over 65 or a 60% VA-disabled veteran, you are eligible for the free State Parklands Passport. This sticker, which attaches to your windshield, exempts the holder from the entry fee at all state parks. It is good indefinitely, but you must obtain the passport yourself. Bring identification that shows your birthdate to any state park or to the Parks and Wildlife Headquarters at 4200 Smith School Road in Austin.

The department's newest discount program is the Texas Conservation Passport. You will pay an annual fee for the sticker, but it will waive all entry fees and give you discounts on camping. For more information on this program, see the next appendix, "Texas State Parks."

Appendix D. Texas State Parks

Texas has an excellent system of state parks offering camping, fishing, hiking, boating, and tours of historical sites. Facilities range from those with hiking trails, golf courses, and cabins to others that are largely undeveloped and exist as an example of how the region once looked.

There are four classes of parks, with different entrance and camping fees. "Statewide Favorites," including Garner State Park near Uvalde, are most expensive, with a summer rate from June through August and a winter rate a few dollars cheaper. "Popular Retreats," the second class of parks, includes places like Blanco State Park and Inks Lake; these have a higher admission on weekends. "Quiet Getaways," including Enchanted Rock and Lost Maples, also have weekend and weekday rates, but they are slightly cheaper than the "Popular Retreats." Finally, "Overlooked Treasures," including Goliad and Lockhart, maintain the same low rate throughout the week.

Although this new price structure seems complicated, there is one thing to keep in mind: All rates are remarkably low. Admission price for an entire carload does not exceed $5 at any park, even on weekends. Campsites with water and electricity never top $12. Screened shelters range from $15 to $18 a night. Admission prices at most historic sites run only a few dollars.

Reservations, up to 90 days in advance, are recommended for overnight facilities. (Reservations at Castroville's Landmark Inn may be made 12 months in advance.) Credit cards are not accepted. Pets are permitted if they are confined or on a leash shorter than six feet.

For travelers 65 years or older (or those with at least a 60% VA disability), there is the State Parklands Passport. This free windshield sticker permits free entry into any park.

If you visit state parks frequently, consider purchasing a Texas Conservation Passport, which is renewable annually. It provides free entrance into all parks as well as discounts on all campsites and overnight facilities. With it, you receive a newsletter of upcoming events, a directory of access conditions to special wildlife management areas that require a Conservation Passport, and access to guided tours. The Conservation Passport can be purchased at any state park, at the Smith School Road headquarters in Austin, or by mail (4200 Smith School Rd., Austin, TX 78744). For more information, call (512) 389-4901.

For more information on Texas state parks, call the Texas Parks and Wildlife Department at (800) 792-1112 Monday through Friday during working hours, or at (512) 389-4890 in the Austin area.

Appendix E.
Guide to Tex-Mex Food

You'll find Tex-Mex food everywhere you go in central and south Texas. It's a staple with all true Texans, who enjoy stuffing themselves at least once a week with baskets of tostadas, the Mexican plate (an enchilada, taco, and rice and beans), and cold *cerveza*. Unlike true Mexican food, which is not unusually spicy and often features seafood, Tex-Mex is heavy, ranges from hot to inedible, and can't be beat.

CABRITO—young, tender goat, usually cooked over an open flame on a spit. In border towns, you'll see it hanging it many market windows.

CERVEZA—beer.

CHALUPA—a fried, flat corn tortilla spread with refried beans and topped with meat, lettuce, tomatoes, and cheese.

CHILE RELLENOS—stuffed poblano peppers, dipped in batter and deep fried.

ENCHILADA—corn or flour tortillas wrapped around a filling and covered with a hot or mild sauce. The most common varieties are beef, chicken, and cheese, and sometimes even sour cream and shrimp.

FAJITAS—grilled skirt steak strips, wrapped in flour tortillas. Usually served still sizzling on a metal platter, with condiments (pico de gallo, sour cream, cheese) on the side.

FLAUTAS—corn tortillas wrapped around shredded beef, chicken, or pork and fried until crispy. May be an appetizer or an entree.

FRIJOLES REFRITOS—refried beans.

GUACAMOLE—avocado dip spiced with chopped onions, peppers, and herbs.

MARGARITAS—popular tequila drink, served in a salted glass. May be served over ice or frozen.

MENUDO—a soup made from tripe. It is most popular as a hangover remedy.

MOLE (pronounced "MOLE-ay")—an unusual sauce served over chicken enchiladas. Made with nuts, spices, and chocolate.

PICANTE SAUCE—a Mexican staple found on most tables. This red sauce is made from peppers and onions and can be eaten as a dip for tortilla chips. Ranges from mild to very hot.

PICO DE GALLO—hot sauce made of chopped onions, peppers, and cilantro, used to spice up tacos, chalupas, and fajitas.

QUESADILLAS—tortillas covered with cheese and baked. A main dish.

156

SOPAPILLAS—fried pastry dessert, served with honey.

TAMALES—corn dough filled with chopped pork, rolled in a corn shuck, and steamed. Served with or without chile sauce. A very popular Christmas dish.

TORTILLA—flat cooked rounds of flour or corn meal. Used to make many main dishes, and also eaten like bread along with the meal, with or without butter.

VERDE—green sauce, used as a dip or on enchiladas.

About the Authors

John Bigley and Paris Permenter are a husband-wife team of travel writers. Longtime residents of central Texas, they make their home in the hill country west of Austin near Lake Travis.

John and Paris write frequently about Texas and other destinations for numerous magazines and newspapers. Their articles and photos have appeared in *Reader's Digest, Americana, Texas Highways, Flower and Garden, Wildbird, San Antonio Express-News, Denver Post, Oakland Tribune,* and many other publications.

Order Form

ORDER DIRECT—CALL (800) 877-3119 OR FAX (816) 531-6113

Please rush the following book(s) to me:

_____ copy(s) **DAY TRIPS FROM SAN ANTONIO AND AUSTIN** for $8.95 plus $2 shipping

_____ copy(s) **DAY TRIPS FROM KANSAS CITY** for $8.95 plus $2 shipping

_____ copy(s) **KANSAS CITY GUIDE** for $7.95 plus $2 shipping

_____ copy(s) **KANSAS CITY CUISINE** for $12.95 plus $2 shipping

_____ copy(s) **MEMPHIS CUISINE** for $12.95 plus $2 shipping

_____ copy(s) **NASHVILLE CUISINE** for $12.95 plus $2 shipping

_____ copy(s) **SAN DIEGO CUISINE** for $12.95 plus $2 shipping

_____ copy(s) **DALLAS CUISINE** for $12.95 plus $2 shipping (available September 1993)

_____ copy(s) **BRANSON COOKIN' COUNTRY** for $9.95 plus $2 shipping

METHOD OF PAYMENT

_____ Enclosed is my check for $_____ (payable to TWO LANE PRESS, Inc.)

_____ Please charge to my credit card: _____VISA _____MasterCard

Acct. # _____

Signature _____

SHIP TO: _____   **GIFT/SHIP TO:** _____

_____   _____

_____   _____

_____   _____

_____   _____

_____   **FROM:** _____

MAIL COMPLETED ORDER FORM TO:

Two Lane Press, Inc. ● 4245 Walnut ● Kansas City, MO 64111